UFOS OVER MAINE

CLOSE ENCOUNTERS FROM THE PINE TREE STATE

Nomar Slevik

Schiffer Publishing Ltd®

4880 Lower Valley Road • Atglen, PA 19310

Dedication

For anyone brave enough to share their story...
and for those who could not.

Schiffer Books are available at special discounts for bulk purchases for sales promotions or premiums. Special editions, including personalized covers, corporate imprints, and excerpts can be created in large quantities for special needs. For more information contact the publisher:

Published by Schiffer Publishing, Ltd.
4880 Lower Valley Road
Atglen, PA 19310
Phone: (610) 593-1777; Fax: (610) 593-2002
E-mail: Info@schifferbooks.com

For the largest selection of fine reference books on this and related subjects, please visit our website at www.schifferbooks.com
We are always looking for people to write books on new and related subjects. If you have an idea for a book, please contact us at proposals@schifferbooks.com

This book may be purchased from the publisher.
Please try your bookstore first.
You may write for a free catalog.

Acknowledgments

My interest into the UFO phenomena began at a very early age and never could I have imagined that a decade's worth of research would turn into this work. Books that stand out amongst the best, which captivate a reader, are only that way because of a good editor. I would first like to thank my editor, Dinah Roseberry, for being so understanding to the growing pains of a new author and who made this book come to life.

My loved ones are the only people who seem to understand the importance of my strange passion in life and I think about you all often and with fondness.

Lastly, I would like to thank the numerous eyewitnesses, interviewees, and research organizations who, without your experiences nor a place to report them, this book could not have happened. NUFORC and MUFON have stood the test of time and have investigated the very cream of the UFO top and I am humbled for your assistance with this writing.

For anyone brave enough to share their story. . . and for those who could not.

It is time for the truth to be brought out. . . Behind the scenes high-ranking Air Force officers are soberly concerned about the UFOs. But through official secrecy and ridicule, many citizens are led to believe the unknown flying objects are nonsense.

Admiral Roscoe Hillenkoetter
Director of the CIA (1947-50)
in a letter to Congress, 1960

CONTENTS

SECTION 1:

INTRODUCTION ... 7

Northern Maine Strangeness . . . 10

A Starting Point . . . 15

SECTION 2:

ABDUCTIONS AND THE MEN IN BLACK ...29

A Case for David Stephens . . . 32

Doctor's Warning . . . 36

The Allagash Abductions . . . 40

SECTION 3:

MILITARY FALLOUT ...44

The Loring Air Force Base Incidents . . . 46

Brief Reports of UFOs over
Brunswick Naval Air Station . . . 52

SECTION 4:

CASES FROM AROUND THE STATE ...56

A UFO Over Starks . . . 56

The Reiff Encounter . . . 61

The Timber Lake UFO . . . 63

Franklin County Lights . . . 64

Lights Over Industry . . . 66

10 Years in North Whitfield . . . 68

The Glowing Light . . . 70

Shots Fired! . . . 73

Looking Inside . . . 74

The Bucksport USO . . . 75

A UFO Caught on Video in East Newport . . . 77

Police Witness . . . 80

Crop Circles in Gardiner . . . 81

Fire in the Exeter Sky . . . 83

The Curious Case of Wendy C. Allen . . . 85

SECTION 5:

CONCLUSION ...88

Additional Information and Reports . . . 90

UFO Factoids . . . 92

National UFO Reporting Center . . . 94

Mutual UFO Network (MUFON) Maine Report Index . . . 94

Glossary . . . 138

Bibliography . . . 141

Index . . . 144

INTRODUCTION

The research conducted for this book was a task first accomplished by simply having open discussions with Mainers from around my current residence (Bangor), a few quick searches on the Internet, and referencing my own library of Maine books on the paranormal. As time went on and the research went from weeks to months to years, I could not believe the enormous amount of data for sightings and encounters with UFOs, extraterrestrial entities, and Men in Black in the state of Maine. A daunting task for sure, and even though I was overwhelmed, I scoured every report, every story, and every encounter that I came across. The longest part of the research came after combing through the large amount of data was trying to determine the best stories and encounters to relate in this writing.

Who knew that Maine was home to alien abductions, UFO confrontations with the military, and more sightings than possible to count? Maine, paranormally speaking, is known more for hauntings than it is for UFOs, for strange beasts in its vast forests than for extraterrestrial encounters. Maine authors such as C.J. Stevens, Marcus LiBrizzi, Michelle Souliere, Stephen King, and many more, have all written about the paranormal side of Maine to some degree. Stevens' book, *The Supernatural side of Maine*, is filled with many tales of UFOs and extraterrestrial, biological entity encounters. Librizzi's books are packed with tales of hauntings throughout Maine, past and present. Souliere's book, *Strange Maine*, mentions Bigfoot, the Turner Beast, and the Loup-Garou (The French-Canadian name for werewolf). And King has written numerous stories about UFOs in Maine—granted, all have been tall tales of sci-fi nightmares including, *The Tommyknockers, Dreamcatcher, Beachworld, The Lonesome Death of Jordy Verrill,* and more.

As you read through the different sections of the book, I hope you will share the same enthusiasm and wonderment of these encounters, just as they unfolded before me, slack jawed over every word.

Tonight, just after you put down this book, step outside and look towards the stars. *Observe* the sky instead of just *seeing* it. Look towards the horizon and take note of the constellations. Look for planes low in the sky, and notice the satellites much higher in the atmosphere. Check for the International Space Station (there are numerous apps for your smartphone that track the International Space Station) and notice shooting stars. When all have been accounted for, as much as is possible, perhaps a light in the sky will be much too bright. Perhaps the object you are witnessing is too low and silent to be a plane. Perhaps this is *your* encounter—a story of your own to tell. It is a rarity and the feeling can seem unnerving, but it will be replaced with fascination and excitement. I hope it happens for you.

The truth is that every state has its own weirdness just waiting to be found by those who are interested. However, Maine itself has a singularity that captivates the hearts and minds of people from all over the world.

Michelle Souliere

Strange Maine

NORTHERN MAINE STRANGENESS

Before my UFO life was birthed wholeheartedly, its earnest beginnings started with the unassuming world of children's ghost stories and being a firsthand eyewitness to some unexplained phenomena. I thought every seven-year-old boy checked out UFO books from their elementary school library. Mine had about four that I took out every month until the day I started high school. As it stands now, my apartment is littered with books by authors such as Raymond E. Fowler, Jenny Randles, Whitley Strieber, John A. Keel, Erich von Däniken, and Stanton Friedman. Besides those are scraps of paper scribbled with terms such as "manna machine" and "vimanas" (look them up), as well as copies of *Fortean Times, Fate* and *UFO Magazine*, with all the spines horribly creased and, unbeknownst to the casual observer, all dog-eared on the UFO articles of the month. I sky watch constantly, almost too diligently to the point where my roommate will walk by and say, "It's just a plane." To which I scoff and retort, "I know!"

I'm obsessed with Indrid Cold and flying humanoids, with the alien skeleton from Mexico and the Flatwoods Monster (clearly an alien encounter). I thought "rods" were interesting and I'm still concerned about chemtrails. The point being that my eyes are to the sky and my heart is filled with all things paranormal.

I was born in Fort Kent in December of 1977, and I lived in the small northern town bordering Canada until the age of nine. My hometown is most famous for hosting the CAN-AM dog-sled race, housing the Olympic biathlete training center, home to the Fort Kent Blockhouse, and of course, it is the northern most point of U.S. Route 1, which stretches approximately 2,400 miles to Key West, Florida.

During my time in Fort Kent, I was too young to learn of all the paranormal happenings around my state that are so familiar to me now. Of course, there are the UFO incidents, which occurred at Loring Air Force Base, the Allagash Abduction case that was famously researched by Raymond E. Fowler. There are the heartbreaking stories of the Haynesville Road, which continue to occur to this day, with the road even receiving its own country music ode. The numerous Bigfoot sightings throughout the area's vast forests also continue to be reported. There's the "Maine Monster" from Turner, and let us not forget the innumerable amount of hauntings with stories passed down from generation to generation.

As a child, my mother would tell me of the paranormal experiences she and some of her sisters had as teenagers living in Eagle Lake and St. Francis. My mother lived in the humblest of homes, large to me at the time, but as an adult, its size and appearance shrunk and withered with time. The home ballooned and ached with each sibling born, my mother being number five of eleven.

The upstairs of that home was the starting point of my mother's brief paranormal experiences. She related a story to me about my aunt, who was fourteen or fifteen at the time of the encounters. Almost nightly, my aunt would go to bed; after a few minutes, she would feel someone lay down next to her, on the bed, and she could hear "its" breathing. Hearing that story as a child, I was fascinated by its strangeness. I wanted to hear more stories, but more importantly, I wanted my own experience. Little did I know I would have my own story to tell, a story about a home in St. Francis. Years later, I told my mother about my experiences at Mrs. Cyr's House.

Mrs. Cyr, or Mimi, as we affectionately called her, lived in a quaint, ranch-style house located just on the other side of Fort Kent, heading out of town towards Allagash. The small town of St. Francis is about three hours north of the famed Haynesville Road, right at the border of Canada, where the St. John and St. Francis Rivers meet. From the mid-1960s to the early 1970s, Mrs. Cyr's house was like a second home to my mother and she even looked to her as a maternal figure.

One night, while staying at Mrs. Cyr's home, my mother was upstairs trying to get some sleep, but a rainstorm raging outside kept her awake. Eventually, Mrs. Cyr came upstairs to bed and tried to settle in for a good night's rest. Approximately thirty minutes went by when, all of a sudden, the hallway light turned on. Almost immediately Mrs. Cyr called out to my mother and said:

Something bad must have happened.

Finding this statement a bit odd, my mother inquired as to why she would say such a thing. Mrs. Cyr's explanation was that it was a way of letting us know that someone's life had been taken. That thought weighed heavily on my mother's mind, who found little rest that night. Once morning arrived, the news was buzzing all around town. A young man, well known in the community, was out driving in the rainstorm. He'd lost control of his vehicle and died on the scene. It can only be assumed that the young man passed when the hall light turned on the previous night.

Throughout the following years, my mother always kept in contact with Mrs. Cyr, and as a family, we would all take weekend trips to her house. She was the kindest and most gentle elderly woman this side of the St. John, and she loved it when we would come for a visit. Typically, my father would do some yard work for her while my mother sat inside and had coffee and chatted. My sister and I usually played outside on her large wrap-around porch, watching dad sweat during the summer heat.

As most children do, eventually, I would have to go to the bathroom, which was located upstairs past Mrs. Cyr's bedroom. Usually, this was not a problem, but at Mrs. Cyr's house, I would experience a lot of anxiety about having to go upstairs to use the bathroom. Downstairs was always filled with sunlight and cheer, but upstairs was different. I used to hate getting the urge to go to the "little boy's" room. Sometimes I would try to get away by peeing outside, but I was usually told to "get inside and go proper."

This was the point where I found myself at the foot of the stairs, staring up into a much darker, foreboding upper level of the house. From this vantage point, everything appeared to have a bluish hue to it. I always thought this was strange and wondered why nobody else in my family noticed it.

I started my ascent and instantly the stairs creaked—not helpful, but I forged ahead. Once arriving upstairs, it felt like you were being watched or that there was some sort of presence—not to mention that you were greeted with an old picture of Mrs. Cyr's husband. I'm sure he was a kind soul, but the picture used to scare the hell out of me and I felt as though he was the presence upstairs. Quickly, I would run to use the bathroom, fake washing my hands, and run back down stairs. If I had taken any longer, I know that I would have seen "it" or "him" or whatever was up there.

Since then, the strangeness of Northern Maine has never worn off. I do have a few fond memories, though I recall being more scared than happy. Eventually, though, I moved on. In 1987, my family and I moved to the small coastal town of Northeast Harbor. I was a long way from home, I missed my friends, and contrary to my parents' beliefs, we stuck out like sore thumbs on such a small island.

I was about to start my fourth grade education in an unfamiliar school with unfamiliar people, so the paranormal was the last thing on my mind. Years went by without incident. The only memory I have of anything paranormal came from a friend living in Lamoine.

It was August of 1996; I was a recent graduate of Mount Desert Island High School and was eagerly waiting for September to arrive, as I was moving to Boston, Massachusetts. While hanging out one night with my friend, he told me a story about a family that his mother knew. The family was driving along the shore around the Frenchman's Bay area when they noticed a bright light in the sky. Thinking the object was a helicopter, but with a light much too bright, they rolled down their windows for a better look and were startled as no sound was heard. The light eventually reached the shore, dimmed, and an oval object was observed. It was estimated to be about seventy-five feet off the ground. The object crossed the road and disappeared over the tree line. At the time, I scoured the *Bar Harbor Times* and *Ellsworth American* for any mention of it, but none was found.

I was far removed from my Northern Maine roots at this point, but the paranormal was at the forefront of my mind. The strangeness of Northern Maine would creep into my subconscious from time to time, which allowed sensitivity to the paranormal to be shaped lovingly in my heart and in my mind. This would eventually breed, what feels like, an innate need to help others afflicted with circumstances potentially deemed paranormal. A need so genuine that it transcended ridicule. I have Northern Maine to thank for helping shape my outlook.

A
STARTING
POINT

———

Northern Maine, despite its sprawling wilderness and beautiful landscapes, could be considered an extremely harsh environment to raise a family, especially with an economy that is anything, if not, difficult to endure. It has been said, and it has been my experience, that the people who live there are the only ones who can, and that sentiment is worn with pride in the hearts of those people and my respect is given without question.

If you have not had the good fortune of experiencing a Northern Maine winter, I for one can safely say that the fortune is truly all yours. These are winters with record-breaking snowfalls and a cold so harsh it can take a good thirty minutes to warm all appendages thoroughly, once you've finally made it indoors.

The coldest temperature ever recorded in Maine was actually reported quite recently. Minus 50 degrees was observed on January 16, 2009 around 7:30 a.m. at the Big Black River near Depot Mountain in northwestern Aroostook County. A frigid day for sure, not unlike the bitter cold I experienced one night as a child at my first home on Main Street in Fort Kent. My family and I lived in a duplex that my father owned. We had a large backyard and a hill on which to sled during the winter.

One night, during one of those winter months, I was sound asleep in my small corner bedroom that faced the St. John River. Rustled out of bed, I awoke to my father carrying me downstairs where my mother was waiting with my coat, hat, mittens, and boots. As she struggled to dress me, I recall the excitement in which my father was speaking:

C'mon Trish, get him dressed, quick!
You have got to come see this!

My sister was standing at the door, dressed for the weather and clearly annoyed at being woken up at such a late hour. I made a silly face at her, which my mother quickly stopped me from doing so no brother/sister fight escalated to the point of us being dragged back to bed. With boots finally tied, my father scooped me up, and the front door creaked open with a sense of awareness, almost hinting to all of us that the outdoors was the last place we needed to be on such a frigid night. Ignoring the door's plea, my face immediately reddened and burned as my father carried me down the front porch and onto the frozen tundra known as our front yard.

"Look...," he whispered and pointed towards the night sky.

Scared to open my eyes for fear of them watering and freezing instantly, I looked up. I do not know if it was the bitter cold, or the beauty of what we call the Northern Lights, but I lost my breath. I stared in awe, too young to understand and process the kaleidoscope of colors I was witnessing. After what seemed like an eternity, my family and I walked back inside, numb from the cold and awestruck. That experience taught me something at a very early age as I was starting to understand that the world I knew was something much larger and much more mysterious than that of the world I knew before that night, which only consisted of my living room, backyard, and school. It felt like the world was revealing its strangeness to me and I was fascinated by it.

A First Experience?

Fast forward a few months and you will find my family and I in the mid-thaw of what was to become an interesting month of April. The worst of the winter was behind us and dirty snow littered our driveway and front yard, proving that another Maine winter had been survived.

Day turned to night and I was at play in my bedroom knowing that I would soon be told that bedtime had come. Sure enough, the stairs creaked and my mother's voice provided me with my evening reminder. I obliged and drifted off to sleep. Without warning, a loud bang echoed throughout the house. My eyes popped open and darted around for an explanation, but none was immediately found. Then, as my body and I adjusted to the stillness of the night, I started to hear the light taps at my window.

"Rain," my young mind observed. My eyes followed my thought and when they reached the window, a quick flash lit up the night sky. A thunderstorm was upon us.

I knelt on my bed so I could look out the window and watch the lightning. I sat there for a long while watching the sky flicker like a tourist's flashbulb trying to capture one of our moose onto celluloid. Another loud crack of thunder accompanied an equally disturbing lightning bolt, which seemed to slice through a now oddly dense late night sky. The last thought I had before falling asleep was the image of that jagged yellow line of electricity that appeared to show itself much longer than the usual millisecond of visibility.

Morning arrived and I could hear my parents chatting downstairs. I got up and ran to the bathroom, then headed back to my room for some early morning playtime. As I was walking back towards my room, I could see the grey, cloud-filled sky through my bedroom windows. But something wasn't right. From my vantage point, the middle and left-most windowpane had a peculiar image in it. It looked as though I had gotten into some hobby paint and flicked a brush dipped in yellow at my window. As I got closer, I could see clearly that there was no paint or any other foreign substance on the glass. The color was etched into the sky itself. I studied this oddity for a moment and then went to get my father.

When we finally arrived at the window, my underdeveloped logic had trouble explaining what I saw. I turned to point, but the phenomenon was no longer there. I tried to tell my father that a lightning bolt had become stuck in the clouds from the storm the night before, but that didn't seem to make any sense to him. I tried harder to make him understand what I had seen, but he could only nod in agreement, as most adults do when a child is trying to make a silly point. He did manage to inform me that there was no storm the night before. Upon hearing this, I pleaded and explained about all the loud bangs and cracks of thunder that I had heard; that too was met with a loving stare and the nodding of hapless agreement. For a long time after that strange sighting, I assumed that I had simply witnessed another fascinating weather or environmental phenomenon, much like my experience with the Aurora Borealis months earlier. But as time went by, and even to this day, I wonder if that was the first time I had observed a UFO.

Grainy

The next strange anomaly that occurred over a long period of time started when I was a young child, and is not something that I have heard of very often. I have no recollection of when it started or what the catalyst could have been. During the evening, and especially in the late night hours when there were no lights on in the house, I would see everything in a grainy black and white. I would liken it to watching a recorded VHS copy of a black and white movie, or maybe, and more accurately, fine rain. I never really considered this as something supernatural, but I do think it is noteworthy as it is a bit odd. Also, I never thought that this was a weird thing or even worth mentioning while I was growing up. I just assumed it was like that for everyone. As a child, why would I think any differently?

It wasn't until I was much older that a friend of mine brought it up to me in conversation. This was about seven or eight years ago while I was talking with him on the phone in my apartment, which, at the time, was located on Saint John Street in Portland. As most of our conversations go, it took a turn towards the paranormal. We shared whatever was on our minds at the time. I have since forgotten the specifics of the original topic, but he did mention something that was quite surprising. He proceeded to tell of a friend of his whom, as a child and even as an adult, would see everything at night as grainy black and white. I stopped him in mid-sentence and told him that I had the exact same experience. Mine had a little twist, which I will explain in more detail later. But yes, I knew exactly what he was talking about. To this day, he still experiences this "fine rain" or "pixilation" as he explained to me:

I will tell you that I see the world like this all
of the time. It's one of those things, like a fine
rain. You do not see the drops unless you look
for them. . . you just accept that they are
there. In the dark, it is less subtle; the "pixels"
move and I seem to be able to affect that
movement.

For me, this seemed to stop around 12 years of age or so. After some further research, I happened upon an online message board dedicated to the phenomenon. I even spoke with a local ophthalmologist/optometrist (who would not give me permission to use his name), but briefly stated:

It's most likely neurological.

Then he politely ended the conversation. More alarming is that a few forum members to the website, *Visual Snow or Static* (http://thosewithvisualsnow. yuku.com/) state that they have tried to get their vision issue diagnosed and were told that they had conversion disorders.

The Diagnostic and Statistical Manual of Mental Disorders (DSM-IV) defines conversion disorder as a condition in which:

• One or more symptoms or deficits are present that affect voluntary motor or sensory function suggestive of a neurological or other general medical condition.

• Psychological factors are judged, in the clinician's belief, to be associated with the symptom or deficit because conflicts or other stressors precede the initiation or exacerbation of the symptom or deficit. A diagnosis where the stressor precedes the onset of symptoms by up to 15 years is not unusual.

• The symptom or deficit is not intentionally produced or feigned (as in factitious disorder or malingering).

• The symptom or deficit, after appropriate investigation, cannot be explained fully by a general medical condition, the direct effects of a substance, or as a culturally sanctioned behavior or experience.

- The symptom or deficit causes clinically significant distress or impairment in social, occupational, or other important areas of functioning or warrants medical evaluation.
- The symptom or deficit is not limited to pain or sexual dysfunction, does not occur exclusively during the course of somatization disorder, and is not better accounted for by another mental disorder.

While I realize that this is a possibility, most of these people, along with my friend and I, assert that we were not suffering from mental disorders. However, most of us were distressed to varying degrees; being dismissed by science is typical.

The twist that I experienced along with my nighttime vision color and quality issue was the appearance of lines. These lines were constantly twisting and changing, forming squares, rectangles, and turning into themselves only to re-form instantly. The only comparison I can think of is someone using an Etch-A-Sketch™ with extreme speed to form lines, squares, and longer lines, then erasing them and starting over again. I saw the shapes right in front of me at night while lying in bed staring at the ceiling or wall, and even when I had my eyes closed. These experiences stopped at the same time the black and white graininess went away and I have no explanation for it.

Hauntings Aplenty

The next major paranormal experience occurred in 2004. I was living in Portland and working for a television network whose headquarters were housed in an old building on Custom House Street, often dubbed, "The old W. L. Blake building."

One day, while digitizing a video for the editors I worked with, I was sitting in my office when I felt someone walk into the room. My back was to the door and I was expecting my visitor to vocally make him- or herself known. Just as I was about to turn around to see who walked in, I felt a tap on my shoulder and I spun around, startled...no one was there. I got up quickly and looked in the hallway, but no one was there, either.

About a month later, I was working very late and I had all of my recorders running at full capacity. There was a lot of white noise, humming machines, and a headache slowly taking over an otherwise peaceful night. Since my recorders had about an hour and a half to run through their program, I decided to take advantage of the large flat screen TV near the editor's bay to relax and watch some television. It was about 11:30 p.m. and the restaurant on the first floor was just about to close. About ten minutes into my program, I heard the door from the stairwell open, and then close. I thought this was odd because those doors were locked at night. I assumed the task had been forgotten and some of the restaurant crew, or mischievous teens, were having a bit of fun coming in and out of the offices. As I got up to investigate, I started hearing footsteps from the floor above me, which was also a part of our offices. But this wasn't just footsteps on creaky boards in an old building; it was stomping around and was extremely loud and a bit frightening. I made my way to the stairwell door to see if I could see anyone on the staircase. The stomping got louder and appeared to follow wherever I went.

As I approached the stairwell door, the stomping above me stopped and it was eerily silent. About thirty seconds passed. I was ten feet away from the door when a flurry of sounds came from above. The upstairs stairwell door flung open and I could hear it hit the wall with a loud crack, most likely causing damage to the drywall. Then I heard something run down the stairs, getting closer to where I was, and the feeling was ominous. I felt that whoever or whatever was coming down those stairs knew I was there, knew who I was, and was going to harm me.

I was frozen, too scared to move. As the sounds got closer, I became more and more afraid. Just as the sounds were approaching the door...silence befell the building. The ominous feeling fell by the wayside and I felt like I snapped out of some sort of daze. I decided to venture into the stairwell and head up the stairs. Sure enough, there was a broken piece of drywall on the floor with a hole in the wall to match. But the door was locked.

Confused and panicked, I ran back downstairs fearing that the other door was locked, too...it was. The doors hadn't been left unlocked after all. My thoughts then changed to all of the running equipment in my room and how I was going to get back in. Fortunately, I had my keys with me. I was able to make my way to the street, unlock the front door, and use the elevator to get back upstairs.

With my work completed and no other activity occurring, I left the building with a personal experience that I couldn't quite shake and told my coworkers about the next day. Some were skeptical, some were surprised, and others had noticed a presence in the building as well.

Fast forward a few years and I was living in Freeport, renting a house located on Old Brunswick Road, which is off Route 1. I loved living there, but the house had its fair share of problems. As soon as you walked in the front door, you were greeted by a tin ceiling and one large, white ceramic sink in the largest kitchen I have ever seen. That was great, but upon deeper investigation, the house was filled with insects, disjointed corners, and collapsed and poorly repaired interior ceilings. The upstairs was no better. The bedrooms had scuffed floors, marked walls, and a very small bathroom. Despite all of its flaws, it was my home for three years and I enjoyed every minute of it.

While the house could be creepy on its own, it had a few helpers along the way. Every time you left the living room to go upstairs, you had to walk through the dining room. Every time I did this, I became mildly frightened. It came on all of a sudden, though it did not last long, usually dissipating once I returned to the living room. For a while, this both confused and frightened me until I figured out that it was most likely a fear cage. The term "fear cage" as defined by Long Island Paranormal Investigators (http://www.liparanormalinvestigators.com/definitions.shtml) is:

> A term used to describe a confined area such as a walk in closet, hallway or basement with very high EMF readings. The combination of being close and confined with in an area of strong EMF often brings out extremely great feelings of uneasiness, anxiety, paranoia and/or uncontrollable fear. When this occurs the best thing is to quickly and calmly leave the area and go to a more open area with lower EMF.

The electrical wires running through that house had not been updated for some time and the landlord had told us how the wiring ran from the kitchen through three-quarters of the walls of the dining room and then to the electrical box. With the dining room bearing the brunt of the wiring, the electromagnetic fields recorded in that room alone were off the charts. The electromagnetic field (EMF) meter was pegged. With that said, we had one anomaly solved when another one sprung up.

I was sitting on my couch one afternoon drinking water and watching television. Needing to leave for a moment, I placed my half-full cup of water on the side table that was next to me and proceeded upstairs. A few moments later I returned and sat on the couch again. While watching the television, I reached for my cup without looking. My hand had trouble finding my drink so I looked over and was shocked to see that the cup was gone. My heart felt like it skipped a beat and I gasped a little. Everywhere my eyes darted, no cup was seen. I got up, bent down to look under the table...and there it was, sitting next to the far, back right leg of the table. I had to get down on my hands and knees and crawl underneath the little table to finally reach my cup, which was still half-full. After getting over the shock of the incident and knowing I was home alone, I thought it was the coolest yet oddest thing that had ever happened at the house, until few months later.

My roommate was out for the weekend and I was home alone. No big deal usually, until the thunder, wind and rain started; the house lost power so I decided to hunker down in the living room with the cats and enjoy a good book or two. I had four candles casting those cartoon, devilish-like shadows across the living room walls and ceiling, the book *Wiseguy* by Nicholas Pileggi in my hands, and two cats snuggled and sleeping next to me on the couch. As I reached the part of the book where the character Henry was "exporting" cars to Haiti, I heard a horrible crash come from the kitchen that startled not only me, but the cats as well. They were suddenly awakened and staring wide-eyed at the door to the kitchen. I looked at the door, hesitant to investigate. It stood there mockingly, daring me to unlatch it from the wall's clutches and peer into the kitchen for the source of the terrible crash. But I just sat there, staring at the door. No vertigo, no creepy violin music, just the cats and me, fully awake and scared.

I slowly closed the book; I even recall becoming a little annoyed because I forgot to save my place first. I placed it on the coffee table and whipped the blanket off me. I stared at the door again and finally stood. The cats seemed to watch me in awe, proud of their father's courage, I imagined. I made my way to the door, turned the knob and, as if on queue, the door creaked, and a dark kitchen was revealed.

I was standing in the kitchen now, my eyes needing no adjustment to the darkness. I just kept looking at the mess around me wondering what the hell had happened. In the middle of the kitchen, my roommate and I kept an island, filled with knives, fruits, paper towels, etc. At this point in time, the island was free from our kitchen garnishes and, to my surprise, all littered the floor of the surrounding area. Closest to the door were the knives, which had breached their wooden container. I started to pick them up when I began having a "bad feeling."

I'm sure I was just shaken by the strangeness of it all, but I had to get out of the house. My cats were nowhere to be found, though—I'm sure hiding under dad's bed was where they were. I grabbed a coat, went outside and locked the door behind me. I sat in my car for sometime, just staring into the woods, contemplating what took place in my kitchen. Maybe the wind had become so strong and I had left a window open, and it hit just right, but no, I had not left a window open. Perhaps it was an animal, like a squirrel or a raccoon, frightened by the storm that had made its way into the house and jumped onto the island and scattered everything. Sure, that was possible, but I had never seen anything larger than a tiny field mouse in my house, but yes, it was possible.

I related the story to my roommate, sister, and colleagues. All of them agreed that the animal theory was possible, but not probable. I was left with a personal experience, a good scare and a creepy story for the upcoming Halloween season. Little did I know but a new mystery would soon be upon us.

On the evening of October 31, 2006, my sister, roommate, and I decided to do a paranormal investigation of the Freeport house to see if there was anything to the few, minor experiences that I'd had. I rounded up the digital camera, digital voice recorder and we shut off all the lights. We went from room to room, asking questions, taking pictures and having a bit of fun. With the interior of the house fully investigated and nothing coming up on the digital voice recorder, we decided to investigate one more area... the utility room.

The utility room was attached to the house between the main part of the house and the garage. You actually have to enter this room to get to the interior. We used the room for storage, but it looked as though the original owner may have used it as a makeshift woodshop, complete with a base for a lathe, clamps attached to long tables, and numerous amounts of tools and saws.

Since my roommate refused to go into that room at night, my sister and I ventured inside. She was asking the questions and holding the digital voice recorder, while I was about ten feet in front of her taking pictures with the digital camera. We must have been in there for five minutes or so when I started getting that "bad feeling" again. I assumed it was high EMFs, especially with all of the exposed wiring in that room. I did notice that my attention was focused in a particular corner of the room, far left, so I started snapping pictures. My "feeling" didn't last long, so after about fifteen minutes, we stopped our investigation, and headed back inside. We wanted to check the digital voice recorder for any potential EVPs (electronic voice phenomena). We all settled into the living room and the three of us huddled around the little voice recorder and pressed play.

"Is there anyone here with us tonight?" said my sister. "What is your name?" she added. Jason Hawes would have been proud. "Were you the one who moved Paul's cup of water?"

And just after that question, the three of us heard a male voice say, "Robert."

As if choreographed, all three of us jumped back, shocked to hear a voice that was not our own.

"Rewind it!" I yelled.

"...cup of water?"

{silence} "Robert."

My roommate, being the skeptic that she is, was extremely surprised. "That is not your voice!" she said.

I could only nod back with the biggest smile on my face. I brought the device to work and had my colleagues listen. I wanted their impression and if they thought it was me. After the first playing, my boss jumped back and started rubbing his arms trying to extinguish the immediate onslaught of goose bumps. Second time through, my good friend and colleague stated, "That doesn't sound like you at all." Again, I was all smiles.

I tried countless times to get "Robert" to talk to me again, but I was unable to document anything else. I talked to my landlord to ask if there was a former tenant named Robert, but she said no. I did a search of town records and I did find the name "Robert Jameson" dated 1814. He was a surveyor of roads. But I could not tie him to the actual location, just the general area. I may not have been able to get to the bottom of our invisible house guest, but it turns out, that was the least of our excitement.

Light in the Sky

The following year, as late September approached, along with its cooler temperatures, my roommate arrived home from work one night, slightly panicked. I heard her running up the front steps, slammed the front door, and ran into the living room, out of breath.

"What the hell is wrong with you?" I asked, confused by her actions.

"There's a light in the sky. I swear to crap I just watched it as I drove up the driveway. It's headed towards Brunswick," she squeaked out between breaths.

I just sat there, stunned. My roommate is the biggest skeptic I have ever met, and for her to be telling me this, I didn't know what to think. I looked at her a bit longer, blinked a couple of times, and then stood up and raced outside. I scanned the sky for any light source other than the moon and the annoying streetlight that kept crossing my field of vision. After thirty seconds, I fumbled for my car keys and drove off toward the town of Brunswick, not five minutes up the road. I kept an eye to the sky but could not see what had gotten my roommate so excited. The lights of town were going to be coming up soon and would diminish my view of the pristine night sky. I came upon a Bed and Breakfast that I had driven by a million times before, but for the life of me, I could not tell you its name. What I did know was that across the road from this nameless B&B was a field with a full clearing and view of the sky. I pulled over and got out...nothing. I watched longer, knowing that any second a full-blown close encounter of the first kind would happen. Ten minutes went by...nothing. I started to get cold...nothing. My head was on a constant swivel, north, then east, south then west...nothing.

I reluctantly got back into my car and left the area, arriving back home a few minutes later, defeated and disappointed. Walking up the steps of the porch, I could see my roommate through the large paned kitchen window, making dinner for herself. She saw and greeted me at the door,

"Well?!" she said, just as excited as when I'd left earlier.

"Nothing," sounding deflated. "I couldn't find it."

She observed the light at the tree line on the right side of the road heading towards Brunswick. She saw it quickly, and it was big. She described it as odd shaped and knew that it was not a plane or the large cargo vessel that we see flying from the Brunswick Naval Air Station. Now the Naval Air Station is not an innocent bystander in all of this, either. Numerous UFOs have been spotted in its vicinity, even around the same time as the Loring Air Force Base incident, but we will get into those stories in much more detail later.

A little more than a week after my roommate's first sighting, I was upstairs using the computer when I heard the front door slammed close, again. I entered the hallway just in time to see my roommate run up the stairs.

"It's back again and it's right across the street!"

I did not hesitate this time and quickly made my way down the stairs and out the front door. As soon as I reached the steps, I looked across the street and saw two red lights with a white light in between them hovering about 100 feet over my landlord's house. I looked at it, trying to make sense of it, knowing fully well that it had to be a helicopter and that it would start moving at any moment, but it wasn't a helicopter. There was no sound at all. The lights did not seem independent of each other, but rather part of a solid object. It just hovered there as if allowing me to see it.

About two minutes passed when I finally realized that a picture was needed. In my haste to get outside, I had forgotten to grab my camera. I did have my cell phone on me, and pulled it out to snap off a picture. But I was too far away and the phone's camera was far too inferior to capture anything more than a faint red streak surrounded by darkness.

As I finished putting my cell phone away, all the while not taking my eyes off the strange lights, it finally started moving...slowly, making no sound. The lights moved diagonally up about thirty feet and then it stopped again. Another minute passed and the lights started moving in a level trajectory, heading towards Brunswick. I got in my car and started backing down my driveway. I pulled onto Route 1 and I had already lost sight of it. Mad at myself for taking my eyes off the lights, I drove a little faster, heading towards the B&B, positive that I would see it there. Again, nothing. I sat in my car for nearly an hour and no other lights were observed. When I got home, my roommate must have seen the wide-eyed excitement on my face and she simply said:

"Told ya!"

Why UFOs

With all of my experiences and interests in the paranormal, why focus on UFOs, aliens, and abductions? With countless books, documentaries, television programs, and movies, what could I possibly have to contribute to this already heavily researched phenomena? Some authors have had firsthand encounters that warrant serious consideration, while others are subject matter experts. So, why bother? Why this book?

I am fascinated with regional retellings of stories rarely heard. Of stories never shared. People who are in need of validation through an open mind where conscientious scrutiny replaces judgment. Simply put, I want to help who and where I can. I want to be an advocate, a listener, a helper. I want to be a conveyer of engaging strangeness to anyone with an open mind and a willingness to listen. If you are that person, thank you.

SECTION 2

ABDUCTIONS AND THE MEN IN BLACK

J. Allen Hynek, an astronomer, professor, and most notably, ufologist, was recruited as a scientific advisor to the U.S. Air Force to conduct UFO studies. His first assignment was Project Sign, which started in 1947 and ended in 1949. Project Sign then turned into Project Grudge (1949-1952), which became Project Blue Book (1952-1969).

Hynek started his research as a skeptic and debunker, but after the countless reports, he was unable to debunk an average of three percent of the claims he encountered. He began to see that there was much more to the unidentified aerial phenomenon than he originally thought. His skepticism, thanks to an open mind, was always objective. His research led him to the claims that could not be dismissed or debunked. He eventually created the original classification system of UFO and alien encounters (animate beings). His classification system included:

Close Encounter
of the First Kind

A sighting of one or more unidentified flying objects.

Close Encounter
of the Second Kind

Observing a UFO, and associated physical effects from the UFO.

Close Encounter
of the Third Kind

Observing "animate beings" in association with a UFO sighting.
There have been additions, not done by Hynek himself, but most notably
by his close associate Jacques Valle. The latter's additions include the
rarely referred to: Distant Encounters described as:

1.
Nocturnal Lights

Unexplainable light sources at night.

2.
Daylight Discs

Generally oval or disc shaped metallic
in appearance sighted during the daytime.

3.
Radar/Visual

Unidentified "blips" on radar screens that
coincide with and confirm simultaneous visual sightings.
In addition to Hynek's original
"close encounter" classifications is:

Close Encounter
of the Fourth Kind

Alien abduction, or direct communication with an animate being.

The major obstacle versus the Close Encounter of the Fourth Kind (CE4) theory is the almost total lack of direct evidence. The scientific community thrives on this type of evidence—evidence that Dr. Roger Leir, a doctor of Podiatric Medicine, would suggest we already have.

• A defense worker experiences bizarre radio-like noises coming from inside his jaw. Dental X rays reveal a small triangular object of unknown origin.

• A woman witnesses a UFO one night in the San Fernando Valley. Ever since, she has carried a small, unidentifiable object implanted in her leg.

• A young boy witnesses a glowing, hovering object one night in a potato field. Years later, during a routine X ray, doctors find a mysterious metal object buried deep within his flesh.

Dr. Leir, after receiving his degree in 1964, became Director of Residency Training at the Simi Valley Doctors Hospital. He and his team claimed to have removed more than a dozen alien implants from abductee sufferers.

I realize that the alien abduction phenomenon can be hard to believe, but consider the following stories of compelling and truly bizarre encounters from the pine tree state and what full disclosure could potentially mean to all of us.

A CASE
FOR DAVID
STEPHENS

The Lake Thompson area: home to quaint, waterside cottages, and all the fishing one would ever need. However, ask David Stephens, and he may have an entirely different opinion of Oxford County.

On October 27, 1975 (the same exact date as the Loring Air Force base incidents; about 300 miles north in Limestone), David and his roommate, Glen, were in their Norway home when a loud bang or some kind of explosion was heard outside. The two men ran to see what had disturbed the stillness of a late fall night, but found nothing out of the ordinary.

On a whim, it is told, David and Glen got into their vehicle and decided to drive towards the Lake Thompson area in Oxford. Following Route 26 for less than a mile, the men claimed that some sort of force field "enveloped" their car. At this point, it is reported that the car began operating all by itself. They said that the vehicle reached speeds of over 100 miles per hour, eventually stopping in a clearing in Poland.

While there, they described seeing headlights from a truck or some type of large vehicle. David said that he and his roommate were feeling a bit relieved to have someone else nearby, but this good feeling was short-lived. The lights they observed began to rise out of the clearing and into the air toward the tree line. The two friends quickly realized that these lights were obviously not attached to a truck or even a helicopter, but rather, a long, multicolored craft that hovered above them. Fearing for their lives, David and his friend sped out of the clearing and back onto the road.

They did not have a chance to drive very far when they noticed a different light had begun to follow them. It was bright white, and it seemed to overtake them. Suddenly, everything became silent, there were no more lights in the sky, and they were no longer driving, in fact, they were parked near another body of water, eventually identified as Tripp Pond. David and Glen were perplexed as to how they'd gotten there. An odd feeling overcame David who looked up and saw the same multicolored UFO again. Glen saw it, too and noticed two other smaller crafts with white lights that hovered low over the pond. At this point, the two crafts were observed releasing some sort of smoke or fog over the pond, eventually making its way to the car with the two men inside.

Left staring blankly and confused by what happened, the men noticed that it was finally daylight. The roommates drove back to their home feeling not only exhausted, but also confused and lethargic. Their eyes and necks burned. David even claimed to have had several loose teeth from the encounter.

The next morning David woke up to a pounding at his door. Exhausted and noticeably weak, he answered. David described that the visitor was not your typical, friendly Maine neighbor, but a man dressed in black formal wear complete with sunglasses and a military haircut. He demanded to know if David saw a UFO last night. This seemed odd to David and the visitor seemed to be in a hurry and pressed David for an answer. Too tired and confused to verbally answer, David indicated, yes, by nodding his head. The Man in Black barked back at the exhausted Norway resident saying it would be in his best interest to keep his mouth shut about what he saw. With that, David's visitor left.

Despite the unusual warning from the man in black and farcical claim of all that he witnessed, David decided to report the incident to the police. Not really knowing what to do with such a claim, his incident was forwarded to noted Maine UFO researcher, Shirley Fickett. It was recommended by her that he see a doctor and undergo hypnosis sessions. A meeting by Shirley was set up between David and a general practitioner and hypnotist,

Dr. Herbert Hopkins. Dr. Hopkins held about eight sessions with David over a five-week period. Each session included the doctor, David, David's parents, and Shirley.

During the sessions, David described being abducted and taken aboard a UFO by what is now commonly referred to as the "Greys" alien race. David said his roommate was never taken aboard and was left in their vehicle. Dr. Hopkins discovered that the aliens had examined David and numerous samples had been taken from him including, skin, hair, and blood. David also claimed that the aliens took a button from the jacket he had been wearing at the time. David, while under hypnosis, informed the doctor that the aliens had told him that this encounter would be forever buried deep into his subconscious.

A few weeks after David started his hypnosis sessions, an officer had come forward claiming to have seen a UFO that same night over Norway.

Officer Lloyd Herrick of the Norway City Police Department on patrol that night claimed the following:

> I was patrolling about one o'clock in the morning and drove out to Norway Lake west of town when I looked up and just saw this thing coming over the pines. I've never seen anything like it before. I stopped and got out of my cruiser and watched it. It was shaped like a short cigar and had two red lights on it, one in front and one in back. The middle part was black. It couldn't have been more than 800 feet above me. It wasn't going very fast. In fact, pretty slow. I must have watched it for at least a minute as it passed over Norway Lake and headed right in the direction of Norway. It must have passed right over the town. I called the Sheriff's Office on my radio and said, "I don't want to sound corny but have you had any reports of UFOs?" The dispatcher said something about what had I been drinking. I was so amazed by this thing! It made no sound.

It wasn't a plane. I said to myself, "Well, son of a gun! I've seen something I've never seen before!"

Before Shirley Fickett or Dr. Hopkins could have any further sessions with David, or interview Officer Herrick fully, a strange incident occurred at Dr. Hopkins' home in Old Orchard Beach.

DOCTOR'S
WARNING

In 1976, general practitioner and Old Orchard Beach resident Dr. Hopkins experienced the Men in Black phenomenon firsthand. On September 11, 1976, the doctor's wife and two sons had gone to the movies while Hopkins stayed home. He was quietly reading in his home office when he received a peculiar phone call. The caller identified himself as a member of the New Jersey UFO Research Foundation. The gentleman on the phone asked Dr. Hopkins if he could discuss the "Stephens Case" with him. The doctor obliged and invited the man over. After the telephone conversation ended, Hopkins walked down the hallway to turn on the porch light, so his visitor would be able to find his way to the front door. As the doctor approached the door, his unfamiliar guest was already waiting to be let inside.

> I saw no car, and even if he did have a car,
> he could not have possibly gotten to my house
> that quickly from any phone.

The stranger, now inside Dr. Hopkins' home, appeared short in stature, was dressed in a black suit, hat, and tie, with Hopkins noticing that the clothes appeared brand new. The guest made himself comfortable and removed his headwear, upon which, Dr. Hopkins observed that this person was completely devoid of all hair on his head, including eyebrows and eyelashes. He was pale with extremely flush lips. At one point during their conversation, the doctor watched as the stranger unconsciously wiped his mouth "smearing" his red lips, implying that this odd man in black was actually wearing lipstick. The doctor also noticed that his guest had a very unusual manner of speaking, though he couldn't put his finger on it, but it didn't seem foreign, more mechanical.

The stranger then started questioning, not just the Stephen's case, but alien abductions and UFOs in general. The Man in Black stressed the importance of forgetting everything about the Stephens' case, destroying his cassettes, notes, and having no more sessions or dealings with David Stephens. He explicitly ordered the doctor to destroy a letter written by Shirley Fickett, that the doctor had received earlier in the week. Dr. Hopkins wondered how this man could possibly have known about the letter.

The events that followed these demands rattled Dr. Hopkins like nothing before. The odd visitor told the doctor that he had two coins in his pocket. A bit shocked, Hopkins said yes, he did indeed have two coins in his pocket. The stranger told Hopkins to hold one of the coins out in front of him in his opened hand, which he did. Suddenly the coin started changing colors and became somewhat transparent, and then the coin disappeared completely! The strange man then said that the coin would never be seen again. He further insisted that if the doctor continued his research, that the same thing would happen to the doctor's heart. Oddly, the stranger's speech slowed down like a record player in slow speed.

He rose unsteadily to his feet and, little by little, said, "My energy is running low... Must go now... Goodbye."

Hopkins saw him to the door and watched him falter as he descended the stairs, placing both feet on each step before attempting to negotiate the next one.

As Dr. Hopkins watched the mysterious man walk away, he saw what he described as a bright white light, not in the sky, but in his driveway. When Dr. Hopkins looked away from the light to find out where his visitor had gone, the visitor was nowhere to be found. Looking back to the driveway, the light was gone. Moments later, back inside his home, the doctor burned all notes and tapes related to the Stephens' case. According to his wife, when she arrived home, the doctor was sitting at their kitchen table, with every light in the house turned on and a gun in his hand.

As stated earlier, the doctor's family had been at a movie that night. His wife had gone with their oldest son and the son's wife. The younger son had gone separately with his girlfriend. Here is what they experienced while there:

An Aftermath to the Man in Black

While at the movies in one car, the doctor's wife looked out the window to the heavens and observed what she felt might be a UFO hovering. She, at the same time, felt an anxiety for her husband back home with the desire to return. They stayed for the entire movie, although she expressed this desire to her son. In the other car, at the outside movie, sat the younger son and his girlfriend. For some unknown reason, [son's girlfriend] was also picking up anxious feelings about the doctor during their time at the movies.

Dr. Hopkins reported that for a brief time, he had nightmares and that the family experienced odd phone calls with unexplained sounds on the other end of the line. But that wasn't the only strange encounter or visitor to the Hopkins home.

Approximately two weeks later, while Dr. Hopkins was away at work, two more strangers came knocking. His son, John, and John's wife, Maureen, were there at the time and answered the door. Before them stood what appeared to be a man and a woman dressed in black with a look of constrained pain on their faces. Stumbling as they entered the home, the unknown couple settled into the living room. Awkwardly, the man in black asked a question about what people talked about, as if ignorant to human and social interactions. John and his wife simply looked at each other, confused by the question, and then their guests began acting crudely.

The male visitor began touching his female companion intimately and asked John whether he was fondling her correctly.

Startled by this act, John and Maureen became quite uncomfortable. John was about to ask the odd pair to leave when he was distracted by the telephone ringing, subsequently leaving Maureen to fend for herself. Alone with John's wife, the man then asked how she was put together and if she had any pictures of herself in the nude. Appalled by the question, but too dignified to answer, she sank in her chair when John came back into the room. Almost immediately, the couple in black excused themselves and left the Hopkins' home. John and Maureen could only shake their heads in disbelief and were relieved once the couple had left.

The doctor's story has almost become urban lore in some circles, especially since his death in 1987. With the recent passing of Shirley Fickett, the story sensationalized itself, leaving new generations to discover the high strangeness once reported from Old Orchard Beach.

THE
ALLAGASH
ABDUCTIONS

———

In the summer of 1976, four men ventured north from their college in Massachusetts to the beautifully pristine Allagash Wilderness Waterway in Northern Maine for a long trip of fishing, camping, and living off the land. Late in the afternoon of their first day, four friends, Chuck Rak, Charlie Foltz, and identical twin brothers, Jack and Jim Weiner, canoed to the Mud Brook Campsite of the waterway; it was here they first noticed something in the sky. Another camper nearby saw the odd light first, which prompted Jim Weiner to grab a pair of binoculars:

> and focused on the "star" and immediately realized it was not a star. It was an object only a few miles away and approximately 200 feet above the treetop level.

A few nights later, during a canoe trip to Eagle Lake, the incident was subsequently forgotten. The four friends tried their hand at some night fishing, since their daytime trout attempt yielded no results. Before leaving, Jim commented about the fire they'd made:

> The fire was so large that I was very worried
> that it would start a forest fire.

With no concerns, the rest of the group suggested that it will help them find their way back to the campsite in the dark. Convinced, Jim and the rest got into their canoes and headed out onto the water. While out on the lake, the men, again, observed a light in the sky. They all noticed that it was much too strange and it appeared out of place. It was lower in the sky than the first light they'd seen earlier in the week. This object was not hovering miles away; this time it was hovering a few hundred yards away, close to the tree line. Described by Chuck Rak:

> I became completely absorbed in observing
> the object to the exclusion of everything else.
> I could see a fluid pulsating over the face of
> the object as it changed color from red to
> green to yellow-white.

What followed can only be described as one of the best documented claims of alien abduction since the Betty and Barney Hill encounter in New Hampshire, the Travis Walton abduction, the Brooklyn Bridge abduction, and the Whitley Strieber case.

A fascinating aspect to their story is, at the time, not one of the four men realized that an actual abduction had taken place. From their perspective, they observed the light, and a few moments later, they watched as it gained speed and zipped away. Once arriving back on shore, they discovered that the large campfire that they had built before leaving was now barely smoldering, indicating to all of them that a significant amount of time had passed. It wasn't until the innumerable nightmares, strange ailments, distant memories, and about twelve years had passed that their incredible story would be fully unearthed.

Fast forward to 1988, and we find Jim Weiner at a UFO conference in Massachusetts. One of the speakers, Raymond E. Fowler, whose UFO research has spanned close to forty years, was approached by Jim. He went on to explain the medical issues he'd had to deal with since the abduction. Fowler, fascinated by the story, decided to take on the case.

In 1989, Fowler officially filed for a full investigation with MUFON (Mutual UFO Network), including investigators David Webb and Anthony Constantino. These men were known for Close Encounter of the 3rd and 4th kind specialties, and Constantino was an expert in hypnotism, thus finally revealing the full story of the Allagash abductions.

All four men underwent numerous hypnosis sessions with Mr. Constantino. It was revealed that the four abductees had somehow been transported to the UFO from their canoes. It is assumed that a beam of light, which was witnessed by the men, was how this transportation occurred. Jim stated during a hypnosis session:

> The beam—it's going to get us! It's right there right behind us. I know there's no use. It's no use paddling. The beam! It's got us! It's there. We're in it!

Once on board the unidentified vessel, the men succumbed to some sort of mind control or manipulation by very odd-looking animate beings (aliens). Forced to remove all of their clothing, the four friends were then led to a plastic seating area. This is where a lot of the preliminary examinations took place. The gentlemen were poked and prodded, after which, they were again placed on an examination-type table.

> ...they were made to lie on a table where each was examined by a number of strange hand-held and larger machine-like instruments that were lowered over their bodies.

Like the David Stephens' case, these four men were also the victims of having samples taken from them, including blood, sperm, skin, and more. Once the examinations had finished, the four friends were ordered to dress and enter the beam of light. The men were dazed and utterly confused, but eventually found themselves on shore at their campsite. The large fire had now turned to dying embers. The sight of the almost extinguished campfire bewildered the men as they thought only fifteen to twenty minutes had elapsed.

Throughout the rest of their lives, after this event, the friends and brothers continued to have odd experiences. Jack Weiner claimed that he and his wife were simultaneously abducted from their own home, in 1988. Not long after the 1976 abduction, Jim Weiner was diagnosed with temporolimbic epilepsy. Jim's doctors asked if there was some sort of event that could have triggered this medical issue. He revealed to the doctors his abduction story and was immediately advised by them to seek out the help of a UFO investigator.

Raymond E. Fowler wrote and released a book about the incident titled, *The Allagash Abductions: Undeniable Evidence of Alien Intervention*. The book was popular and received much fanfare, including a documentary and two major segments from the television programs, *Sightings* and *Unsolved Mysteries*. In 1998, WCSH 6 out of Portland aired a show about the incident as well, under the moniker, *Maine Mysteries*. During the episode, it was revealed that Chuck Rak no longer believed that this extraordinary event occurred.

Chuck Rak once believed this happened to him, but he no longer does. Further evidence of this is described by noted author C.J. Stevens,

> The event did not traumatize him, he claimed,
> it was just imagery from a vivid dream.

The four men eventually went their separate ways, though they typically stayed in contact with one another, excluding Chuck Rak. Charlie Foltz is a medical illustrator. Jack Weiner studies the ancient Mayans of Central America and his brother, Jim, works at the Massachusetts College of Arts. Finally, Chuck Rak is reported to be a caricature artist in Vermont. Despite Chuck's denial of the incident, Charlie Foltz summed up their collective experience quite simply and to the point,

> The abduction happened. If you believe, that's
> all right. If you don't believe it, I don't care.
> But it did.

SECTION 3

MILITARY FALLOUT

They are the visible signs of an invisible, parallel world within the universe of aerospace and defense: the classified, or "black," world of secret military programs.

Bill Sweetman | PopSci | 10/1/2006

The Groom Lake Test Facility (Area 51), Edwards Air Force Base (AFB), Holloman AFB, Homestead AFB, Kirtland AFB, Langley AFB, Oakdale Armory, Peterson AFB, Wright-Patterson AFB, RAF Bentwaters (England), Pine Gap Research Facility (Australia), Shahrokhi AFB (Iran) and, of course, The Pentagon, the headquarters of the U.S. military, have ALL been suspect to everything from harboring alien bodies, to monitoring alien communication, receiving constant radar detection of extraterrestrial aircrafts, to the testing and reverse engineering of unidentified aerial propulsion systems. The public awareness of these Air Force Bases and facilities along with their alleged involvement with some very famous UFO and alien encounters is common knowledge within most circles of the paranormal pop culture community. Most famously, there's the 1947 crash in New Mexico, which was immediately confirmed and reported by the military as a crashed flying saucer, then subsequently called a weather balloon; the Rendlesham Forest case involving a landed craft observed and recorded on audio tape by American soldiers and their commander in England; there's the "Battle of Los Angeles" incident where the U.S. military were engaged in a fight with an unknown craft over L.A. for many hours, and, of course, Bob Lazar and the Area 51 whistle blowing. The list goes on and on, but here in Maine, we have our own AFB and Naval Station stories. While not as famous as the incidents listed above, they did receive national attention.

THE LORING AIR FORCE BASE INCIDENTS

Limestone, Maine

On October 27, 1975, Staff Sergeant Denny Lewis was on duty at Loring Air Force Base. It was a typical evening of monitoring base activity when the stillness of the early evening was interrupted at 7:45 p.m.

Lewis reported a red light, about 300 feet off the ground, heading towards the restricted air space of Loring AFB. It quickly became apparent that the light was attached to an actual craft of some sort and the Staff Sergeant immediately became concerned. While Lewis was on the ground, astonished at what he was seeing, another Staff Sergeant, James Sampley, was in the base's control tower monitoring radar, when he noticed an unidentified hit on his monitor.

The radar return approximated that the unidentified aerial phenomenon was then ten miles away from the base. With all attempts failing to contact the craft via military and civilian radio bands, the oddity entered restricted air space. A moment later, the radar returned that the craft was hovering approximately 300 yards over the nuclear storage area of the base.

Not long after all this activity started, the entire base was put on a "Security Option 3" alert status. As soon as this alert went into effect, the UFO was spotted hovering only 150 feet above the base! Base security was visibly monitoring the craft and, as part of protocol, contacted the control tower to get radar confirmation. With the confirmation conveyed, another sergeant, Grover Eggleston, arrived at the control tower and watched as the ship circled the base after its close, 150-foot proximity.

Because a significant breach of security occurred, the base Wing Commander, Col. Richard Chapman, ordered that the entire base be searched for any "persons unknown." During the ground search of the base, Loring requested air support from North Bay, Ontario, and Hancock Field, New York. It is reported that both bases denied sending fighter jets, so the base contacted airport flight services for help on identifying the object and alerted the Maine State Police. The ground search yielded no finds, despite the UFO being observed for over forty minutes.

After the event, Loring AFB contacted Strategic Air Command, The National Military Command Center, the USAF Forward Operations Division, and even the USAF's Chief of Staff to report the incident, even though no further sightings were reported that night.

The next evening, October 28, 1975, at precisely 7:45 p.m., again, Staff Sergeant Lewis, along with Sergeants Long and Blakeslee, observed another unidentified flying object on radar, about three miles away. Eventually, the three men would spot the UFO with their own eyes, after which, Lewis notified base command. After the notification, Col. Chapman decided to try and visually spot this craft for himself, so he set off to the nuclear storage area where he met up with one of the base's security personnel.

Col. Chapman startled the young man as he barked, "What the hell is going on? Why didn't you report this to the tower?!"

The officer stated that the tower *was* contacted. Satisfied, the Wing Commander and the security policeman stood there, mesmerized, watching the object. Not long after this, a second UFO was sighted over the base. This was first acknowledged by Sergeant Steven Eichner and a Sgt. Jones, along with other base personnel.

. . . a silent orange-and-red object shaped like an elongated football hovering over the runway. . . about four car lengths long, solid, with no doors or windows, and with no visible propellers or engines.

The ship was seen just hovering over the base and at one point it just disappeared. Moments later, it was hovering 150 feet over the base's runway. As numerous base personnel looked on in awe, a plan was made to confront the craft from the ground. The men piled into a truck and started driving down a parallel road to the runway, towards the object. Once they reached the turn to the weapons storage area, the craft was approximately 300 feet in front of the truck and reportedly only hovering five feet off the ground. Eichner said later:

> There were these waves in front of the object and all of the colors were blending together. The object was solid and we could not hear any noise coming from it.

Moments later, base security and state police descended upon the runaway to confront the craft. Seconds later, the craft shut off its lights and disappeared.

In two days, the Loring Air Force Base experienced two security breaches. Col. Chapman was not about to let this happen again, so he put in a request for helicopter assistance from the National Guard, who were already stationed at Loring, and because of the previous night's events, the assistance was quickly approved.

The unidentified craft encounters continued for the next few nights with the helicopter crew being called out numerous times to track and identify the object. Time after time, though, when a sighting on base was reported, the helicopter crew spotted nothing. At one point, ground personnel watched as the helicopter and crew were not within 100 feet of this object, yet, radar nor the helicopter crew were able to see the craft.

Base officials, concerned about these breaches of security, were forced to put all bases under their command on a "Security Option 3" alert. Included in that status alert change were, Barksdale AFB in Louisiana, Brunswick Naval Air Station in southern Maine, Fairchild AFB in Washington state, Grand Forks and Minot AFBs in North Dakota, Kincloe, Wurtsmith and Sawyer AFBs in Michigan, Malstrom AFB in Montana, Pease AFB in New Hampshire, and Plattsburgh AFB in New York.

Years after the Loring AFB incidents took place, the son of a previously mentioned security policeman, on site during the nights of the incidents, contacted the website www.rense.com and submitted a letter, further deepening the mystery.

> I was reading your page on the 1975 Loring AFB UFO incident and got a little chuckle. My father was a security policeman with the 17th Security Police Sq, and was on duty the nights in question. For several years after I learned of the incident, my father as well refused to discuss it. About a year ago, maybe longer, he relented and told me what went on the first night. The object in question, he refuses to call it a UFO, was silent. It had suddenly appeared over the weapon storage area and the alert aircraft from nowhere.

This part of the letter confirms the claims from Staff Sergeants Sampley and Lewis, on the first night of the encounters, that the object in question showed an observable interest in the nuclear storage area.

It has been documented countless times, since nuclear technology was born, that there seems to be some type of UFO/nuclear connection. Robert Hastings, who mostly worked as a photographic technician for Northern Illinois University, first began researching this connection due to a 1967 UFO encounter at Malstrom AFB in Montana. He observed 5 UFOs hovering and beaming lights, at what he later found out to be the nuclear storage area of Malstrom.

> The wing commander called up the tower and asked them to verify the light. They immediately denied it. The commander then told the NCO in the tower, "If the eagle on my shoulder sees that light, then those stripes on your damned sleeve better see it too." They immediately, albeit a little dumbfounded, said that they saw

it as well. The whole incident this night lasted some time more and then was over. My dad went back and filled out the log with the entire incident and started a report on it as well.

Again, confirming claims from Col. Chapman and Staff Sergeants Lewis, Long, and Blakeslee that an observable unidentified flying object was indeed on site. Also, it appears that the Men in Black potentially paid a visit to Loring following the incidents. Further research could not produce any other claims of this, but compelling and all too familiar the following seems to be.

That morning a couple of men from the Air Force came up and started questioning everyone who had seen the incident first hand. They were not told to be quiet by these men as they went through the investigation. When they finished, my father said that they came to his duty station to inspect the blotter and related paperwork. They then removed the pages from the blotter and the related paperwork and replaced them with new pages that did not mention the incident. My dad said he knew enough to keep his mouth shut and not ask why they were taking these pages. After that, the matter was closed for all intents and purposes.

Despite the identity, an object was seen in October of 1975 at Loring Air Force Base. Was it simply a helicopter, or perhaps drug smugglers as suggested by some local media?

Some have theorized that the incident was no more than just routine SAC security tests, but is it possible that a truly unidentified aerial phenomenon appeared before military personnel on those nights in 1975? For some, it is not hard to stretch the imagination and believe that something otherworldly took place.

However, some researchers cannot get past the fact that with so many AFB personnel on alert, that not one of them grabbed a camera to snap off a picture of the supposed craft. Regardless, an event clearly took place, an event taken so seriously that an investigation by the Air Force was conducted and eleven other bases were put on alert. But the story does not officially end there.

On October 30, 1975, numerous unidentified aerial objects were spotted in and around the base. Helicopter crews were deployed once again, and told to be looking for other helicopter intruders, i.e., drug smugglers. While many unknown lights were seen in the sky, not one "drug smuggling helicopter" was found.

Soon after the incident, the base had given an official public stance that the previous evenings sightings were helicopters.

Eventually, and under fierce scrutiny, the base reported that during October 25 through to October 30, 1975, the objects observed at Loring Air Force Base....

. . . were NOT identified as helicopters.

BRIEF REPORTS OF UFOS OVER BRUNSWICK NAVAL AIR STATION

February 1966

A light in the sky was observed and was reported to have landed in the woods near the Brunswick Naval Air Station. The object appeared to have green, red and blue flashing lights. After some time, a second object, similar to the first object was observed landing near the same area.

Author Note: As UFO landing reports are so rare, further research into this sighting was very proactive, however, I could not produce a name for the witness, nor any additional information.

June 1971

At approximately 9:30 p.m., an unidentified flying object was reported in the "Cook's Corner" area of Brunswick, very close to the area of the Brunswick Naval Air Station.

> ...a bright light floated slowly along to a point over the sea in Brunswick, Maine. Its lights went out, leaving a glow, then the UFO veered to the SW and shot off at a great speed. It made no discernible sound.

Author Note: The absence of sound is commonly reported during UFO CE1 encounters.

1975

Robert Kinn, a student at Bowdoin College during 1975, had an encounter near the BNAS. Robert and a friend were out on the night of October 27, when they reportedly spotted a very large craft with red and white lights. Being so close to the air station, the students assumed it had to be military in nature. Notice, this is the exact same night as the first Loring Air Force Base incident and the David Stephens' case. Robert Kinn was quoted in the *Washington Post* as stating:

> It came in very low, at treetop level from the ocean. It was like a helicopter, but different. More than twice the size of a normal helicopter. It had red lights and a white light. It would make ninety-degree turns and fly very fast.

Soon after this sighting occurred, the base came to life with police, military personnel, and trucks, apparently trying to track this object. It is reported that the UFO incident over the Brunswick Naval Air Station lasted approximately fifteen to twenty minutes when the craft shot off away from the base heading towards the ocean.

April 2009

An unidentified witness from Brunswick was returning home from work. While getting out of their car and then entering their home, the witness heard numerous dogs barking from around the neighborhood. Thinking this was a bit odd, the witness went back outside and immediately sighted a large orange-colored light in the sky. The light was observed flying from south to north.

> This was NOT an airplane. I quickly ran inside and grabbed my binoculars and my laser pointer. Thru the binoculars it looked no different, so this object, what ever it was, it was big and, pretty far away. I tried to contact it with my laser pointer. It did not respond until I blinked it three times. After I did that the object blinked three times back at me. . . and kept flying on its course! I felt amazed and shocked when it did that. I really didn't know what to think. I watched it until it flew out of sight.

Author Note: Claims of using laser pointers to make contact with UFOs is growing at an alarming rate. The website, YouTube.com has numerous videos of this practice. Please note that pointing lasers at aircrafts is not only dangerous, but illegal.

May 2009

At approximately 9 p.m., two coworkers from Bath Iron Works (BIW) had ended their shifts and were going home for the evening. As they were walking towards their vehicles, one of the coworkers looked towards the night sky and observed a very bright and solid white light.

> We observed this object fly directly over our heads and just kept on going. Don't know exactly how fast, but at least 50-100 mph, not all that fast. The object was completely silent and didn't

fly completely straight. It was kind of "wobbly."
It came from the south and flew north, crossing
the Kennebec river in Bath.

As the object continued its northern trajectory, one of the coworkers decided to leave the BIW parking lot to find a better vantage point so they could continue to observe the sky oddity. What is even stranger about this object is that if it had been just an airplane or a helicopter, it flew directly over Bath Iron Works, which is a General Dynamics company: a company that builds warships for the U.S. Government and has restricted air space. Whatever flew over BIW that night clearly violated that restriction.

March 2011

At around 4:45 a.m., in Berwick, a Cumberland Farms employee, opening the store, noticed peculiar lights in the sky above a building on Allen Street. The lights were reported to the police, but were met with joking speculation. Police Captain Jerry Locke said:

We haven't seen one, but we're always on
the look out for them. There were no crop
circles, we checked.

Townsfolk had their own theories about the lights and their origin. Many thought it was simply a military refueling tanker, especially since one took off that same morning from the Pease International Tradeport at around 5 a.m. After authorities reached out to Pease Community Liaison, Ed Pattberg, it was learned that the tanker did take off at that time, but he could not confirm that it passed anywhere near Berwick.

CASES FROM AROUND THE STATE

A UFO
OVER
STARKS

In November of 1981, Starks, Maine, resident, Kenos Henry, was near Brann Mills Road working at a friends' farmhouse. Looking up at an early evening sky, Kenos spotted a peculiar red light. He watched this light for a moment and realized he had seen it before. However, this time it was much lower and was just hovering. The other two times that he had observed the light he had assumed it was just a satellite, and at first, offered the same assumption this night.

Suddenly, Kenos was filled with terror when the light dispensed a red beam directed at him! He ran into the farmhouse and screamed to his friend,

"Hey, there's a satellite or something up in the sky and it's sending lasers down at me!"

When Kenos ran back outside, he noticed that the light had moved to an even lower altitude. Scared and wanting to leave, he jumped into his car, too fascinated by what he was witnessing, however, to move.

The light kept getting closer and closer; then it zoomed off to the left side of the horizon. As soon as the light maneuvered left, it instantly came back to the right. The light was so low now that Kenos could actually see that this was in fact an actual solid object with a light attached to it.

The object was getting so low that Kenos' dog was barking at it and running around, extremely agitated. Becoming frightened at the events unfolding above him, Kenos decided it would be best to leave the location and start heading home. As he pulled onto Route 43, he could see the UFO behind him. He picked up speed, but the object stayed with him, getting closer and closer to the ground.

Kenos could now see a multicolored light beam being shot toward him from the craft. He remembered that another friend lived nearby and, wanting to get off the road to avoid the beam, he sped up his friend's driveway and flew out of his vehicle and into the house. He described what happened to his friend and visitors there with him.

Not believing the story, they all wanted to look for themselves. Kenos led the charge and they all piled into Kenos' vehicle and headed back towards the farmhouse. As they drove up the road, everyone's head was on a swivel searching for Kenos' light.

They did not have to wait long.

Kenos saw it first, off to the right very high in the sky. It appeared to be the size of a star, but with a reddish glow. Once his friend, Mike Daigle, saw it, he told the carload of friends that it was simply the North Star. Disagreeing almost immediately was Mike's friend, Artie Corrieri, who'd noticed the reddish glow to it and rebutted with a claim of Venus. As this was being discussed, the red light in the sky started to move, first down, then towards the young drivers. It almost seemed as though the light was being passive/aggressive with the group, because as soon as it would come towards the friends, it would then back off.

While Kenos and his buddies were watching the light from the road, Deputy Bud Hendsbee and his wife were also on Route 43, heading towards Farmington. During their drive, nothing seemed out of the ordinary, except when they reached Starks, there was a group of kids stopped in the road, looking up into the sky. Bud slowed down as he approached them and asked if everything was okay.

Kenos replied with, "Hey, don't go up over that hill. There's a UFO up there. Honest to God."

The deputy realized the Kenos and his friends appeared to be frightened, but he was not about to be swayed from driving on the road because of some supposed UFO. He continued on. His wife saw the light in the sky that Kenos must have been talking about. But it was much too high and looked to be the size of a star. They scoffed at the idea of the kids being afraid of a red star and continued on to Farmington to enjoy a meal at a newly opened restaurant.

Heading back to their home in Madison after a very nice dinner, Bud and his wife found themselves, once again, back on Route 43 driving through Starks. As they approached a hill, Bud's wife, Helen, was startled when their vehicle was accosted by a brilliant white light hovering close to the tree line and lighting up the entire area. Bud had to shield his eyes from the light and proceeded to drive up a hill when Helen noticed that the light dipped and started to head right towards them. Concerned with the situation, Bud wanted to get off Route 43. He began backing down the hill when the light dipped again, to about sixty feet over the landscape and settled to the right of Bud's vehicle. In an interview after the incident, Bud discussed his thoughts on the encounter:

> You don't know what this is! It's going to and fro, up and down, floating in the air. You don't know if the thing's going to come through your windshield like a bolt of lightning…Now you're stuck with it! You're stuck with this feeling and you don't know how long it's going to take to overcome it.

Bud felt like the light was watching him as he maneuvered back down the hill, so much so, that he stopped his truck and rolled down the window, sure that it was a helicopter. But there was only silence. This was the first time that the deputy felt truly frightened and finally whipped around his truck and headed for Route 148. It would still get him to Madison and thankfully, the light did not follow them.

While Kenos, Bud, and the bunch finally found their way home, frightened and unharmed, the same could not be said for a 24-year-old woman traveling through Starks that same night. She was on Route 2 heading towards New Sharon, roughly five miles from Starks, when she lost control of her vehicle maneuvering around a curve. The vehicle ended up approximately forty yards into the woods and was not found until morning. But the strangeness of this accident had not yet presented itself.

Leslie Bugbee, who was at the time head of the group Paranormal Phenomenon Research, uncovered some interesting facts surrounding this case:

> First of all, those who knew her said she was not normally a fast driver. State police estimated her speed at 91 miles per hour at the time of impact. Second, she was not unfamiliar with the road; she made the same trip nearly every other day. Third, when she missed the curve and went off the road she left no skid marks, as if she either hadn't hit the brake pedal or hadn't been able to see the road bend. Finally, and most disturbing of all, there is strong evidence that on this dark, overcast night she had been wearing her sunglasses. Tinted, nonprescription glasses— which were always methodically stored in their case when she wasn't wearing them—were found beside the wreck, with blood and skin tissue on them, broken at the left temple.

Despite the odd death reported that night, Bud and his wife eventually decided to report what they had seen that night and called the Waterville Sentinel. What followed were numerous inquiries from news agencies from across the nation. Being a small-town man with a small-town family, this was all too much for Bud. Finally, he said that he and his family were no longer going to talk about the Starks UFO. He just wanted people to forget about it, but mostly, he wanted to stop being bothered. For people who know Bud, they knew that there was just no way that he could forget what he saw, and nor could people just forget the incident. Bud finally realized that this was what happened when a police veteran witnesses and reports an unidentified flying object.

THE REIFF
ENCOUNTER

In 1989, a UFO encounter was reported from Blue Hill Bay by two amateur pilots, Bill Reiff and Randy Rhodes. Reiff, a lawyer from Somesville, and Rhodes, who worked for the Ellsworth Police Department, were flying Reiff's Beechcraft V35 to attend a boat race taking place in Boothbay Harbor. Flying over the Blue Hill Bay area at approximately 4 p.m., the two pilots sighted an unknown craft to the left of them while they were banking.

Thinking that this might be just a reflection of a boat on the water, they watched the object for a little longer. During this time, the craft instantly came to the plane's altitude and simply hovered. Stunned, the two friends could only watch in awe, as the craft instantly moved to their left, started changing in color from a metallic, aluminum silver to a pinkish hue, and then simply hovered again. As Bill Reiff describes:

> It wasn't shaped like any plane I've seen and it was not generating light, but seemed to be reflecting light.

It is important to note, that the pilot and friend described feeling threatened while observing the object, especially when the craft maneuvered to just twenty miles in front of them, revealing it's true size, then eventually shooting off at a high rate of speed. Mr. Reiff explains again:

...in my 300 hours of flying time, I can definitely
say it was bigger than anything I've ever seen
in the air.

After the object left the area, the two friends decided to head back to the Bar Harbor/Trenton Air Field, but the strangeness did not end with the sighting. Reiff reported the encounter to air traffic control in Bangor. They reported that only two aircrafts were captured on radar during that time: Reiff's Beechcraft and another small plane. In addition, once they got back to the car, they found that the radio was dead.

THE
TIMBER
LAKE UFO

In the summer of 1958, Phil Johnson, chaperones, and a troop of boy scouts were on a camping trip to the Timber Lake area of Maine. After setting up camp, the boys, Phil, and the rest of the adults observed a large, disc-shaped craft in the daylight sky. The witnesses observed that the craft was emitting some sort of low hum while moving back and forth, almost floating, just above the tree line. Suddenly, and without warning, the craft flew off leaving the children and the chaperones bewildered.

During the daytime encounter, Phil Johnson managed to take a couple of pictures of the craft. Excited by the sighting, Mr. Johnson reported the event to the Ground Saucer Watch group. He also submitted the photographs to the group, who had the photos analyzed. It was determined that no tampering with the photographs were found and that the witnesses appeared sincere. To view pictures of the Timber Lake UFO, please visit (available at the time of this printing):

Picture 1: http://ufologie.patrickgross.org/pics/timberlake01.jpg
Picture 2: http://ufologie.patrickgross.org/pics/timberlake02.jpg
Picture 3: http://ufologie.patrickgross.org/pics/timberlake03.jpg

FRANKLIN COUNTY LIGHTS

Courtesy NUFORC

Franklin County, typically known for the beautiful landscapes around the Androscoggin and Kennebec Rivers, and the frequently visited Rangeley Lake area, briefly housed numerous, unexplainable lights in February of 2007. The sheriff's office fielded many calls about the lights.

Multiple callers from multiple towns—New Vineyard, Wilton, Phillips, Industry, and around Mt. Abram—called to report bizarre, low-to-the-ground lights.

The witnesses reported seeing approximately seven to eight lights situated low in the sky. Some witnesses stated that they could hear an odd humming sound somewhat like a plane or jet engine, but much too muffled and too quiet to be either of those typical aerial vehicles.

Bill Hoyt, who is the dispatcher to the Sheriff's office of Franklin County, was eventually forced, with all the reports coming in, to call the FAA in Boston to confirm that what people were seeing was a military exercise and to find out if this rural part of New England was registering any hits on the FAA's radar of what people in the community were reportedly witnessing.

They said the only air traffic was a couple of routine air flights at 40,000 feet. I think, personally, most of the time, there's an explanation for everything. But you know, I don't deny the fact that people see things they can't explain. It was kind of odd; all these reports were from different locations at the same time. Maybe it was a meteorite.

No official determination was ever made about the lights.

LIGHTS
OVER
INDUSTRY

—

On November 7, 2006, in the small western town of Industry, Brad Luker observed bright lights in the nighttime sky. Luker, a former naval intelligence cryptography technician, had seen his fair share of military aircrafts. His first thought upon seeing the lights was that they belonged to small plane or more likely, a helicopter. As he was driving at the time, and wanted to get a better look, he rolled down his window and poked his head out; he heard no sound associated with the strange lights.

> It was really bizarre. I've never seen anything
> like it. I do a lot of camping, and I've seen all
> the basic stuff [in the sky]. Most strange things
> in the sky are high up in the air. This was way,
> way down here.

Luker stated that the lights were so low that he actually assumed that there was some sort of gathering or happening at the Industry Town Hall. However, as he drove closer, he could see that this was not the case. He stopped his vehicle, opened his door and gazed at the odd display of lights that were now only 300 feet above him. This time, he did hear a sound emitting from the lights and described it as a quiet jet engine (much like the Franklin County lights).

As he sat there watching the oddity above him, a woman pulled up next to his vehicle, eyes to the sky, Luker asked her what she thought it could be. Her answer was that it seemed like some sort of aircraft was trying to land in the road. Frightened, she drove off, leaving Luker alone with the lights.

Luker said that the lights came to a stop directly over him and that's when his mild nervousness turned to panic. Luker could have sworn it was a spaceship from another world, but followed up that statement by saying that he did not believe in UFOs, or any other sort of paranormal phenomenon.

Maggie Gill-Austern of the *Maine Sun Journal* interviewed former Maine MUFON Director Leland Bechtel about the incident. Bechtel said:

> There has been a lot of activity there in the past. We did an investigation in Farmington a few years ago involving three college students— all very respectable—who saw something somewhat similar to what Luker saw. This thing came directly over them, and stopped, with a powerful floodlight right down on them. Police said it might be a helicopter. But most people can tell when they're seeing a helicopter and when they're not.

After the strange encounter, Luker talked to the police, to which he was told if it was military, they would not be informed as such. *The Maine Sun Journal* even sent an inquiry to the Brunswick Naval Air Station, but their inquiry was never answered. Luker has not been able to find a concrete answer to what he observed that night, but he did have a theory. In the end, Luker said he thinks it was probably a military plane. "But I don't know why they would fly it that low, and I don't know why they would be out in Industry, Maine," he said. "It really doesn't make sense. But that's the only thing I can think of, because I really don't believe in spaceships, or anything like that."

THE
NORTH
WHITEFIELD
SIGHTINGS

A witness, who wishes to remain anonymous, tells of a ten-year affair with lights over her home in North Whitefield.

> …I woke at 3:15 a.m., and looked east out the window and saw a twinkling star in the distance, and I noticed that it had colored lights and it was moving incredibly fast. I thought I was seeing things. It went zipping around the sky.

This was the first of many sightings for this witness, but it seemed as though she was the only person having these close encounters. She could not convince her husband or her son of the lights and crafts buzzing their home on a regular basis, despite accumulating some compelling evidence.

The witness claims to have been cleaning out the home of an elderly couple who had passed away and found a daytime picture of the exact UFO she has seen around her home.

...and found a VERY CLEAR picture from 1967 of a "flying saucer" over our same treetops. I showed it to my husband and said I had seen one in the night some months ago.

(To view this picture please visit: http://www.mufoncms.com/ files/20308_submitter_file1__ufo.jpg.)

A year or so later, during the summer, a triangular UFO was spotted. The witness claims that she only saw the craft briefly, but that it had four large lights attached to it.

I saw colored lights and asked my husband where his binoculars were? He said, "Why do you want them?" I said, "I'm going to look at a UFO that has been bugging me for years. I wish I had a telescope because that thing sat there for 3½ hours without moving much. It moved three times when an airplane entered the airway. Each time, the craft blinked red and green lights more frequently like a normal plane's lights when another airplane would fly near. It would move horizontally and a bit vertically. When the airplane passed, it stopped and remained stationery until the next plane came along. About seventy-five minutes after I spotted this first craft, a second one appeared from the north. About that time, I told my husband there were two of them out there now. He started to take me serious and went out with the binoculars to look and agrees that he's never seen anything like it.

Sightings continue to this day. Convincing others of her encounters isn't a top priority anymore. She knows what she saw and finds comfort in this.

THE
GLOWING
LIGHT

Late one evening, while driving in an undisclosed location in Maine, a glowing light was observed in the sky. Before the light came into view a vibration could be felt. Soon after, their car began to shake. Confused by what was happening the friends became slightly panicked. The experiencer said:

> It was pretty late, like 2 a.m., and there were no other cars around. Suddenly, we feel this vibration. We thought it was an earthquake or something, but the car started to shake, so I slowed down the vehicle.

As the car slowed to a stop, the ground and surrounding area by the front of the car seemed to be lit up by an unknown source. The friends, understandably bewildered, looked towards the front of their vehicle where a glowing light was observed.

> As I'm slowing down, this glowing light flies
> right over the vehicle and comes out right in
> front of us.

The sighting lasted for a long moment, where it was observed making 90 degree turns, maneuvering up and down, then seemed to vanish as it took off towards the stars. During the observation of the impossible movements, a shape seemed discernable and a witness described it:

> ...this thing had no wings. It was shaped like
> an egg and very bright.

Further research into this sighting could not provide any more information, however, another glowing light was observed in Maine in the town of Westbrook.

> My girlfriend, Danielle, and I were outside
> on our back porch smoking a cigarette and in
> the sky we saw a constant white star-looking
> light just coasting from right to left at a very
> good speed, and then it vanished.

Just when they were dismissing the first encounter, possibly thinking they were observing a satellite or any number of other man-made objects, another glowing light came into view—bigger than the last one. This light, too, was moving from left to right, then vanished into the same area as the first light.

The lights, now capturing the attention of the observers, who stayed out on their porch for some time, watching the night sky for any other anomalies. Thinking about what they had witnessed, they figured the glowing light show was done and were about to head inside when a third light was observed. This light was even bigger than the last two, suggesting that it was lower in the sky. As they watched the glowing light, it seemed to get extremely bright and flashed a couple of times just before accelerating at a high rate of speed and vanishing into the night.

...then it flashed a couple of really, really bright lights; then shot across the sky at an unbelievable speed. . . then disappeared.

SHOTS
FIRED!

On March 23, 1965, John King found himself driving on a very desolate portion of highway in Bangor. While enjoying the day's bright blue sky, Mr. King was immediately snapped out of his happy-go-lucky state of mind when he observed a large, silver-domed disk hovering just a few feet over the road in front of him. He reported that the radio turned off all by itself and he had a very strange feeling that something wasn't right, that he might be harmed. Slowing down his vehicle, John became increasingly frightened. He reached for the gun that was beside him, rolled to a stop, put down his window and took aim at the hovering disk before him.

Some reports state that Mr. King took three shots at the UFO, and that he could hear a metallic clang as they ricocheted off the craft. Other reports state that John took aim, firing four shots, missing every time, but on the fourth shot, the UFO shot straight up at an amazingly fast speed.

When John reported the incident to the authorities, they agreed that he did appear visibly shaken and truthful about the incident.

LOOKING
INSIDE

As reported by MUFON in May of 2011, a witness, inside his home at the time, observed two separate lights heading east to west in an undisclosed Maine town. The witness reported that the lights were so low (and headed toward his direction) that he thought that they were going to land right in his driveway.

Going outside for a better look, he could now see that it was two triangle-shaped crafts with lights attached to them and emitting a low hum. A second witness then came out of the house and reported that the two objects hovered very low above them. At this vantage point, the two witnesses claim that they could see inside the crafts! They saw a pyramid-like construction pattern of beams of what seemed like metal. They also observed lights in a geometric pattern and estimated that the crafts were not more than twenty feet wide.

After a few seconds of looking up and into the crafts, the first witness claims that a search light turned on and was fixated on him, then turned off, after which, the crafts flew off at "walking speed" toward the southwest.

THE
BUCKSPORT
USO

———

The serene stillness of a clear winter day in December of 2009 was forever changed for a couple driving from Bangor to their home in Bucksport. Just after crossing the Alamoosook Bridge on Route 46, the couple was startled to see a large charcoal-colored object in the sky. At first the object simply hovered very close to the tree line, where it slowly started moving at a level trajectory, hugging the tree line, but never obscured by it. When the object started moving, the couple was able to get a very clear view of its underside. As the UFO got closer to them, they could see that the craft had kelp hanging off of it and that the underside appeared quite muddy, as if it had been in the water.

Amazed by what they were witnessing, they could only stare in awe, unable to fully comprehend the phenomenon before them. Tim, one of the witnesses, eventually reported the sighting to *MUFON*. Below is what he saw:

> It was very close; it had a white light that switched to orange on its underbelly. The light wasn't a single dot or beam, but was more like a luminous panel. It was grey/charcoal in color. It was not aerodynamic by any means. It did

not make a sound, it did not seem to bother the trees it was "floating" over—I say floating for it was moving very, very slow…maybe 15-20 mph. The bottom or underbelly was smooth and covered with illuminated "panels.

Since reporting the incident to *MUFON,* a number of UFO interest websites have picked up the story, some showing a photo of a perfectly placed black triangle UFO in the center; if not cited on the websites, please know that this photo is actually an artist's rendering of what Tim described seeing that day.

A USO is an Unidentified Submerged Object— essentially, a UFO in the water. The website *Wisegeek.com* defines USOs as:

An unidentified submerged object (USO) is an object that can be detected underwater, but not identified and often not confirmed. In addition to being found entirely underwater, unidentified submerged objects have also been described in transit, hopping into or out of the water, sometimes multiple times. Like unidentified flying objects, their airborne cousins, USOs are a topic of great debate and discussion in some communities, with some people firmly maintaining that they are evidence of alien life or other supernatural phenomena, while others suggest that there are perfectly mundane explanations for such objects.

This is the first and only report of a possible USO reported from Maine. Further research could not unearth any other claims.

A UFO
CAUGHT ON
VIDEO IN EAST
NEWPORT

On March 10, 2009, a local Maine resident captured 17 minutes of what he states are two UFOs flying in formation. The actual videos are still on YouTube and can be viewed here:

Video #1: http://www.youtube.com/watch?v=M3aE9r2UF2E

Video # 2: http://www.youtube.com/watch?v=26Km6yB18V8

The lights that were recorded appear to be in a triangle formation. A similar video was filmed in Arizona; the television program *Fact or Faked: Paranormal Files* on the Syfy Channel recreated the same object with weather balloons and fixed lights on a wooden pallet.

Below is a brief description of the UFOs captured on video in East Newport:

> This sighting was my second sighting on March 10, 2009 at 8:15 p.m. It would fly all up around the sky stop at a certain point in the

air, come towards my house, then fly around
to the front sky—and it kept doing that over
and over.

In watching the video, you can see a light flying erratically vanishing from time to time. During the recording, the witness zooms in on the anomaly, which clearly shows a strobing or pulsing light. At about the 3 minute and 15 second mark of video number 1, the light pulsates again, revealing three lights in a triangle shape. Pausing on this portion of the video you can get a better sense of what the witness is reporting.

The crafts would change up their light
patterns, turn instantly in the reverse direction,
change speed patterns, hover, hover downwards,
and they flew in patterns that I have never
seen any human aircraft fly before.

The second video, filmed the next night, again reveals a triangle UFO. This can clearly be seen at the 3 minute 8 second mark and again at the 6 minute 18 second mark. Excited by the events the witness reports:

…the strobe lights from the craft lit up the
fog and I could see the UFO with 100% up-close
clarity. I could tell it wasn't any man-made
craft.

Both videos total approximately 18 minutes of a flashing light, though moments of fascination occur when the triangle-shaped lights reveal themselves. Comments on the videos claim that the lights are nothing more than an airplane, while others insist it is military, stipulating that reverse engineering of an actual UFO had taken place. Other comments simply scoff at the idea that these lights could be UFOs and seem to take a on a harsh and critical tone. Scrutiny is needed in videos like this, but not ridicule or dismissive judgment. Please view the videos and decide for yourself.

More Maine UFO Videos on YouTube

Acadia National Park: http://www.youtube.com/watch?v=iHRYHDV5fOU

Mid Coast Area: http://www.youtube.com/watch?v=nGNMGtY376w

Harpswell: http://www.youtube.com/watch?v=6Lqml1U6lOI

Harpswell #2: http://www.youtube.com/watch?v=lQOn7tK3lA8

Cape Elizabeth: http://www.youtube.com/watch?v=WhUTtgAko6Q

Orono: http://www.youtube.com/watch?v=LvQ-u_7gCDY

Bath Iron Works: http://www.youtube.com/watch?v=eGomZa7ICik

Maine (general): http://www.youtube.com/watch?v=fgFqYo2pIVI

POLICE
WITNESS

Tuesday, July 11, 1978, numerous residents of the small town of Gardiner saw a brilliant white light shortly before 10 p.m. Three police officers in the area also saw this light and described it as a possible, "...helicopter using a high-intensity spotlight."

Pictures were taken of the object by patrolman Michael Pulire, but have since disappeared. He and the other witnesses described the object as oval-shaped, like a football, but then it changed.

"It changed from an oval to a round circle that seemed to decrease in size," Pulire said.

The officers reported that the craft was flying back and forth and began pulsating. The craft then started descending. As soon as this started, it is said that the object turned red and shot away at high speed. Patrolman William Smith said, ". . . it was a matter of seconds before it became a pinpoint in the sky."

No official determination was made about the lights.

CROP CIRCLES IN GARDINER

Courtesy NUFORC

The town of Gardiner had another case of unexplained phenomena that occurred on August 4th of 2002. At approximately at 2 a.m., a witness awoke to get a glass of water. While doing this, a bright flash was observed coming from the kitchen window. Living across the street from a hayfield, this seemed odd to the observer, as there were typically no lights coming from the field, especially at such a late hour. In her words:

> ...observed a bright white flash of light followed by a small (perhaps flashlight sized) BOL [ball of light] down low over a hayfield across the street from her house. The BOL bobbed around over the crop for several minutes, then seemed to come closer to her location, then "went straight up in a beam of light" and disappeared.

While this was being observed, another neighbor to the hayfield was awakened to the sound of their dog barking at the window. . . which faced the hayfield. Finding this very odd behavior for the dog, the neighbor looked out the window, but saw nothing worthy of the pet's excitement. The dog continued barking for about five minutes.

Eventually a third witness was found, this one being the wife of the owner of the hayfield. She reports that she woke up around midnight and heard an odd sound, presumably coming from the direction of the hayfield. She too, thought this was odd and not typical, as evenings, living across the street from a hayfield, are serene and quiet.

The next day, the incident was reported to NUFORC with an alarming twist: crop circles were found in the hayfield in the morning! NUFORC called in a crop circle investigation team to the area, and later that afternoon, The BLT Research team, whose headquarters are located in Cambridge, Massachusetts, arrived on scene to investigate the incident. A brief description from their report included:

> The plants (grasses and fescue with goldenrod, Queen Anne's Lace, clover and milkweed) were fairly gently laid over, with the thicker-stalked plants such as milkweed clearly showing bending at the base. No broken stalks were found. All plants were swirled clockwise and it could not be determined whether the swirls had begun in the centers or ended there. The initial impression of the crop lay was of fluidity, with a clear undulating character to the flow of downed plants.

A photo of one of these crop circles can be viewed here: http://www.sunjournal.com/files/imagecache/story_large/2009/11/06/ STAweirdcropcircles3110709.jpg.

Additional sources:"A triple-ellipse 'thought-bubble' crop formation found in rural Gardiner, ME, investigated by BLT Research Team Inc." NUFORC.com. N.p., March 2003. Web.

FIRE IN
THE EXETER
SKY

In April of 2013, a young boy was outside of his home, just before dusk, when he saw a disturbing object in the sky and yelled to his father, "Come see this! Just come see this!"

The father, who was in his garage at the time, came running out expecting to see a full moon or perhaps a low-flying plane. When he reached the drive, he saw his wife and son standing eerily still and staring up into the sky. He slowly panned and tilted his head to see what was garnering all of their attention. The father explains in full what he saw:

> I looked up to what appeared to be a fireball in the sky. It wasn't a glimmering star because it was too big and appeared to be moving. It wasn't the aircraft landing lights of a plane because of the size and shape. My thought was it may be an aircraft on fire coming into Bangor International Airport.

Reality set in that this was no ordinary craft and that pictures were needed. The son ran inside to get the camera and emerged moments later. The father took numerous pictures, but being so startled and slightly frightened by what was being observed, a steady hand was hard to come by, so many of the photos were out of focus. At one point, the family was sure that this in fact was an airplane on fire and was actually going to crash in their backyard.

> I did get several pictures of the object. It appeared to almost fade out of sight, but then appeared to come back, getting brighter and larger. My wife asked if it was going to crash and that it was coming right towards us. I snapped a few more pictures and the object appeared to split and disappeared.

After the incident, the Exeter witness uploaded his photos to his Facebook page in the hopes that somebody else saw the same thing that night. No one did... In fact, he was ridiculed by the incident, but is a firm believer in what he and his family saw.

> I put the pictures on my Facebook wall hoping someone else had seen this, but so far I've just been ridiculed. I'm 43 and worked nights for nine years so I've seen shooting stars, aircraft, Northern Lights, etc., but this has me baffled and sends shivers down my spine.

Again, another incident of ridicule for a witness simply reporting what they have seen. My hope is that contentious scrutiny can replace this type of ridicule and close-minded judgment. Claims may seem farcical at first glance, but if we can avoid ridicule, researchers and reporting websites may get more cases of sightings, furthering the field in a positive direction.

THE CURIOUS CASE OF WENDY C. ALLEN

In the summer of 1979, a 4-year-old child named Wendy met what she calls an "amphibious faerie" while in the Ross Forest of Old Orchard Beach. She described it as, a white monkey sitting in a tree; this creature introduced itself to Wendy, advising her to call him Etiole. Her encounters are ongoing.

> ...my contact with him began when I was 4 years old and has continued since then for thirty years till the present day, and he has been throughout my life, the thing by which people judge me.

In the spring of 1983, a loud explosion was heard by many in the small community. Most running outside, a large, oval craft was spotted hovering low in the sky. Interestingly, most people in town just dismissed the event as a military experiment.

These encounters were confusing to Wendy and she could not understand why people had a hard time believing the UFO spotted that spring, and in her tales of Etiole.

> I couldn't talk to anyone about Etiole. No one would believe me, and when I wrote about the real Etiole things got worse…

Autistic and a self-described agoraphobic, Wendy reportedly spent many strange years giving way to her family and the townsfolk religious hysteria about Etiole to the point of church members terrorizing her daily. It has been reported that numerous amounts of small farm animals in her care died at the hands of these people. Not stopping there, these supposed church people vandalized her home, eventually burning it down, leaving Wendy homeless.

Convinced that Etiole would help her through this troubling time in her life, Wendy spent a lot of time with him at his "home" in Bachelder Brook, located in the Ross Forest. They discussed and related horrible tales of being tortured: Wendy by the townspeople and Etiole by a circus freak show some 300 years ago. They also discussed Etiole's capture by Hitler's scientists in the 1930s.

> He has an enormous hatred for the Human race in general, because at some point in his past he was captured and tortured. It's happened to him more than once. The first time it happened was about 300 years ago; he was stuck in some circus freak show thing, where he was billed as a mermaid, due to the fish-like nature of his skin, teeth, eyes, and hands. He was captured by Humans and tortured once again in the 1930s. Again, the date itself is a guess on my part, as he has no concept of dates. He says it was Hitler's scientists who

had him around the time of the Great Wars. I
assume he meant the Second World War, but
his dates are off…

After much internal debate, Wendy decided to start doing things her own way and distanced herself from friends, family, and the town itself. She started her own ministry, speaking about Etiole to anyone with an open mind. She's also an advocate for the homeless, and as of this writing, she states that she is still homeless. I have barely scratched the surface about Wendy and her friend, Etiole. She has written a book about these experiences. The book spans three decades, is hectically paced, and is amazingly engaging. Titled *For Fear of Little Men*, it is a must read for anybody willing to accept, acknowledge, or just be open to the fantastically insane world of Wendy Allen.

Author Note: *For Fear of Little Men* can be purchased on iTunes: https://itunes.apple.com/us/book/for-fear-of-little-men/id468767447?mt=11.

CONCLUSION

The paranormal has been dissected, recorded, observed, scrutinized, scoffed at, dismissed, taken with a grain of salt, exaggerated, and most recently taken more seriously in the mainstream media. With the popularity of paranormal television programs such as, *Ghost Hunters, Chasing UFOs,* and *Ghost Adventures*, we now have what is called the "Para-Celebs"—people like Jason Hawes, Grant Wilson, Bill Birnes, and Zak Bagens, along with the pioneers of the field Tom Slick, Hans Holzer and his lovely daughter, Alexandra, Loren Coleman, Lorraine Warren, and John Zaffis. I could fill an entire book with just the names of the researchers, investigators, proponents, hoaxers, scientists, and skeptics who have the supernatural on their radar. Also, let us not forget that the paranormal not only encompasses spirits and poltergeists, but it whole-heartedly, in my opinion, accepts and includes the Sasquatch, its Himalayan cousin the Yeti, UFOs, crop circles, Mothman, Orang Pendek, Chupacabra, and on and on.

What we are seeing recently is that the paranormal is no longer an after thought. It's not just a fluff piece attached to the last two minutes of a news program during the week of Halloween. It is not the one or two random ghost or alien abduction stories added to a one-hour *Unsolved Mysteries* program. You no longer have to sit in your room and watch old VHS recordings of *In Search Of...* (Although this is recommended.) And certainly, it is no longer the one movie every couple of years taking the paranormal seriously, i.e. *The Exorcist, The Blair Witch Project,* or *The Grudge.* Look at the box office success of such movies as *The Exorcism of Emily Rose, Signs, Cloverfield, Paranormal Activity, The Fourth Kind, A Haunting in Connecticut, The Possession,* and more. What this is doing is allowing the casual observer a glimpse into the passion that researchers and investigators already have for all things paranormal.

At the time of this writing, I am 35 years old and I hope to have another 35 years of experiences, encounters, sightings, etc. I feel fortunate for the brief moments that I have had. I do not expect it to be something special or interesting to an outside observer, but for me, I am grateful to know that not everything is always what it seems to be. Things do go bump in the night. Lights are observed in the sky. Monsters do exist. Varying degrees of belief encompass those statements and with this writing, my hope would be to convey that, at the very least, anything is possible.

ADDITIONAL INFORMATION AND REPORTS

Close and Distant Encounters–Definitions

DE-1 – Nocturnal Light

DE-2 – Daylight Disc

DE-3 – Radar-visual

CE-1 – Light/object in Proximity

CE-2 – Physical Trace

CE-3 – Occupant

Close Encounter of the First Kind

A sighting of one or more unidentified flying objects:

- Flying saucers
- Odd lights

Aerial objects that are not attributable to known human technology

Close Encounter
of the Second Kind

An observation of a UFO and associated
physical effects from the UFO, including:
- Heat or radiation
- Damage to terrain
- Crop Circles
- Human paralysis (Catalepsy)
- Frightened animals
- Interference with engines or TV or radio reception

Lost Time (a gap in one's memory associated with a UFO encounter)

Close Encounter
of the Third Kind

An observation of "animate beings" observed
in association with a UFO sighting.

UFO
FACTOIDS

The term UFO was first coined by the US Air Force in 1952. Since then, the term UFO has been synonymous with alien craft from outer space. Because of this, investigators and researchers of Ufology typically prefer the use of UAPs (unidentified aerial phenomenon). . .

> . . . to avoid the confusion and speculative associations that have become attached to "UFO."

It has been reported that witnessing a UFO, somewhere in the world, occurs every three minutes. Of those, 192 daily are reported, leaving over 100,000 yearly sightings unreported.

A 1991 poll from Roper indicates that approximately 4 million U.S. citizens believe that they have been the victim of alien abduction.

A 1996 Gallup poll states that 71 percent of US citizens think that the government knows about UFOs and are not willing to discuss their unearthly origins.

The website, New Realities reports that:

One in 5 Americans believe in alien abductions. Interestingly, males are more likely to believe in abductions than females. One in 7 Americans say that they, or someone they know, have had an "encounter" with a UFO.

"Airships" have been reported throughout the 1800s, years before the dirigibles of the 1900s were invented. UFOs were reported much earlier than this...in the bible. The first documented sighting could be when the prophet Ezekiel described a "great cloud with fire enfolding itself, a wheel in the middle of a wheel that descended and fired lightning bolts into the earth." The New Realities website also reports:

Winston Churchill reported a strange airship in Kent, England, on October 14, 1912. It was the first case of a UFO being "officially" reported. UFO sightings have been claimed by former President Jimmy Carter, Clyde Tombaough (the astronomer who discovered Pluto), and William Shatner (who claims to have been rescued by aliens who pointed him in the right direction when he was lost in the Mojave Desert).

NATIONAL UFO REPORTING CENTER (NUFORC)

Special Courtesy NUFORC
Peter Davenport, Director

The National UFO Reporting Center (NUFORC) is an organization that reports and investigates UFO/alien sightings or contacts. NUFORC was founded in 1974 by Robert J. Gribble. Since July 1994, Peter Davenport has served as director of the organization.

NUFORC provides a phone number for the general public to report UFO activities that they have witnessed. People may also write or e-mail to report a UFO/alien encounter. NUFORC is known for being one of the first places that many pilots and members of the military report their saightings, alongside police departments, who refer the general public to the organization. You may visit their website at: www.nuforc.org.

State Report
Index for Maine
Each of the following reports will show:
Line 1: the date and time (in military time)
Line 2: the city in Maine
Line 3: the craft shape
Line 4: duration of the sighting
Line 6: a short summary.

2013 - 2010

5/4/2013

Time: 20:00
City: Windham
Craft Shape: Fireball
Duration of Sighting: 2 minutes

───── SUMMARY ─────

Three glowing circular shapes moving together in a semi-formation towards the same direction in Windham Maine.

Author's Note: the sighting described here seems very similar to the UFO captured on video in East Newport.

4/25/2013

Time: 20:45
City: Acton
Craft Shape: Triangle
Duration of Sighting: 4 minutes

SUMMARY

Black triangular, silent craft with 3 white blinking lights on corners and one red one in center.

Author's Note: this sighting is very similar to the object that I witnessed in Freeport in September of 2007, as described in the section, "Light in the Sky."

4/22/2013

Time: 21:00
City: Litchfield
Craft Shape: Triangle
Duration of Sighting: 30 seconds

SUMMARY

A "star" that started moving across the sky.

4/19/2013

Time: 17:00
Place: Route 9
Craft Shape: Other
Duration of Sighting: 1 minute

SUMMARY

Hovering jet liner-like object in daylight.

Author's Note: though a brief description, I did find it noteworthy due to the rarity of daylight sightings. I had a daylight sighting myself in 2006. I was in the city of Bangor, near the town of Hampden, close to the area of Route 1A. I was parked at a self storage unit when something in the sky caught my attention. What I saw looked to be a round, silver ball, high in altitude. It was a very sunny day, and the sun was reflecting off of the object. I briefly walked to the other side of my car when I took my eyes off of the object for a brief moment; once looking back towards the object's direction, it was gone.

4/6/2013

Time: 20:30
City: Patten
Craft Shape: Light
Duration of Sighting: 15 minutes

——— SUMMARY ———

We saw 8 orange lights tracking from north-west to south-east while we were driving through Patten, Maine on Friday, 4/6/2013 at 20:30.

3/26/2013

Time: 5:15
City: Bangor
Craft Shape: Light
Duration of Sighting: 1 minutes

——— SUMMARY ———

Two oval lights appear, hover, and move off to the east.

3/26/2013

Time: 5:00
City: Camden
Craft Shape: Light
Duration of Sighting: 5 minutes

SUMMARY

Large, orange, immobile: suddenly began to move slowly across the sky.

Author's Note: interesting that these last two listings were so close in time, yet so far in distance. Camden is approximately 54 miles south east of Bangor.

2/22/2013

Time: 19:15
City: Piscataquis Co. (T9 R11 Wells)
Craft Shape: Fireball
Duration of Sighting: 45 minutes

SUMMARY

3-4 orange orbs moving across Spider Lake.

2/6/2013

Time: 18:00
City: Skowhegan
Craft Shape: Chevron
Duration of Sighting: 10 seconds

SUMMARY

Large, v-shaped lights hanging in the sky.

1/25/2013

Time: 17:50
City: Hope
Craft Shape: Triangle
Duration of Sighting: 1 minute

SUMMARY

Triangle-shaped group of lights static above a hilltop; it moved, slowly and without apparent noise, in a N/NE direction.

1/10/2013

Time: Unknown
City: Greene/Lewiston
Craft Shape: Cigar
Duration of Sighting: 15 minutes

SUMMARY

Heading south from Greene, Maine to Lewiston, Maine, via route 202/Main Street, one adult and one 17 year old, and I noticed a cigar-shaped object heading vertically in the sky, leaving a short vapor trail, approximately 5 minutes of slow vertical climb, changed direction, and started heading north towards the Leeds Maine area; no engine noise, but airplane in area left very long jet stream, making this object more noticeable. The jet stream was approximately 1/3 the length of the cigar-shaped object as opposed to the planes 4-5x the planes length.

Author's Note: in 2002, a friend of mine observed a cigar-shaped craft hovering near his parents home in the Leeds area. The sighting lasted approximately 5 minutes, and to his knowledge, no one else reported seeing the object.

1/8/2013

Time: 17:30
City: Old Town
Craft Shape: Light
Duration of Sighting: 25 minutes

-------- SUMMARY --------

Bright green light suddenly appeared in the middle of the sky and shot straight downward as fast as a shooting star.

12/31/2012

Time: 23:20
City: Ellsworth
Craft Shape: Fireball
Duration of Sighting: 2 minutes

-------- SUMMARY --------

4 orange spheres flying in diamond formation.

12/30/2012

Time: 16:50
City: South Berwick
Craft Shape: Teardrop
Duration of Sighting: 5 minutes

SUMMARY

Two orange objects flying over Dow Highway in So Berwick, ME.

Author's Note: teardrop-shaped UFOs are rare sightings and are typically observed shape shifting during flight. Also of note is that teardrop UFOs are typically seen pointed down and are described as the size of a small car.

12/25/2012

Time: 20:30
City: South Bangor
Craft Shape: Fireball
Duration of Sighting: 15 minutes

SUMMARY

Five yellow/orange orbs flying across sky at low altitude over 15 minute period seen by 5 people.

12/24/2012

Time: 18:30
City: Bridgton
Craft Shape: Light
Duration of Sighting: 5 minutes

SUMMARY

Several different orange-red pulsing, lighted ball-shaped things that none of us could explain. 5 witnesses.

Author's Note: multiple-witness sightings are also rare: think Stephenville or the Phoenix Lights. With two reports from the same state within one day of each other is even more rare.

12/20/2012

Time: 15:30
City: Lisbon Falls
Craft Shape: Oval
Duration of Sighting: 1-1.5 minutes

SUMMARY

Lisbon Falls, Maine: shiny, oval object.

Author's Note: oval-shaped UFOs strike a chord with UFO researchers and enthusiasts due to the famous Zamora UFO Landing of 1964. Police Officer Lonnie Zamora observed an oval-shaped craft with two entities walking about outside of the object. To read more on the encounter please visit: http://www.ufocasebook.com/Zamora.html.

12/16/2012

Time: 20:00
City: Portland
Craft Shape: Fireball
Duration of Sighting: 3 minutes

—————— SUMMARY ——————

I saw about 9 yellow/orange fireballs traveling slowly in sets of 3, each in triangular formation.

11/28/2012

Time: 23:45
City: Freeport
Craft Shape: Fireball
Duration of Sighting: 1-2 seconds

—————— SUMMARY ——————

Extremely large ball of light streaking from east to west.
   Author's Note: I am not the only one seeing UFOs in Freeport.

12/16/2012

Time: 15:00
City: Houlton
Craft Shape: Teardrop
Duration of Sighting: 30 minutes +

SUMMARY

Strange, cloudy, tadpole-shaped object, dark core, no flames, moving in southern sky with Jet presence seeming to be watching from distance.

Author's Note: another teardrop UFO sighting, this one possibly suggesting military involvement.

11/9/2012

Time: 23:15
City: Lewiston
Craft Shape: Light
Duration of Sighting: 5 minutes

SUMMARY

White light moving across sky that stopped and stayed still.

Author's Note: a typical Maine sighting is seeing a star-sized light moving across the sky, stopping for a moment, then moving again—usually a satellite.

11/5/2012

Time: 2:00
City: Orono
Craft Shape: Circle
Duration of Sighting: 3 minutes

SUMMARY

Bright red ball of light moving at rapid speeds and jets flying towards it.

Author's Note: another suggestion of possible military presence.

11/1/2012

Time: 20:00
City: Waterville
Craft Shape: Circle
Duration of Sighting: 7 minutes

SUMMARY

15 orange orbs in small groups with engine noise.

11/1/2012

Time: 19:35
City: Waterville
Craft Shape: Light
Duration of Sighting: 10 minutes

SUMMARY

8 parallel orange, glowing lights in Waterville night sky.

11/1/2012

Time: 19:20
City: Waterville
Craft Shape: Light
Duration of Sighting: 10 minutes

SUMMARY

Father and daughter witness an estimated 20 orange objects in the night sky.

Author's Note: another rarity in UFO sightings is fleets of UFOs. The amount in these multiple encounters would certainly suggest a fleet. In June of 2004, a massive fleet of UFOs was caught on camera. Skeptics suggest it is nothing more than birds, but witnesses to the event say otherwise. To view a picture of the fleet please visit: http://www.rense.com/1.imagesG/GUAD.jpg.

10/27/2012

Time: 21:00
City: Whiting
Craft Shape: Circle
Duration of Sighting: 10 minutes

––––––––––– SUMMARY –––––––––––

Four red circular lights traveling silently.

10/26/2012

Time: 20:00
City: Woolwich
Craft Shape: Circle
Duration of Sighting: 2 minutes

––––––––––– SUMMARY –––––––––––

Bright light going across the sky, then just disappeared.

10/26/2012

Time: 18:00
City: Enfield
Craft Shape: Fireball
Duration of Sighting: 2 minutes

SUMMARY

Thinking a plane was on fire, until it turned ninety degrees and dissipated to nothing, all in two minutes.

10/19/2012

Time: 2:00
City: Unity
Craft Shape: Circle
Duration of Sighting: 15 minutes

SUMMARY

Circular mass moving through night sky with lights around periphery 02:00 hours in sky over Unity, Maine.

10/17/2012

Time: 19:00
City: Machias
Craft Shape: Light
Duration of Sighting: 3-4 minutes

——————— SUMMARY ———————

Observed solid light heading toward the southwest. Steady, non-blinking, traveling in a straight line. Observed a very quick flash from the east. The steady light made a complete U-turn, then vanished.

10/12/2012

Time: 19:00
City: Shapleigh
Craft Shape: Changing
Duration of Sighting: 5 minutes

——————— SUMMARY ———————

UFO chasing commercial flight in southern Maine!

Author's Note: another rarity in Ufology. There have been some harrowing stories about UFOs tracking commercial flights. Please visit the below link to read about the 1986 Japan Airlines Flight 1628 encounter that happened over Alaska: http://www.ufocasebook.com/jal1628.html.

10/6/2012

Time: 19:30
City: Freeport
Craft Shape: Light
Duration of Sighting: 2 minutes

SUMMARY

7 solid orange lights over Freeport.

9/24/2012

Time: 11:30
City: Wells
Craft Shape: Disk
Duration of Sighting: 1 minute

SUMMARY

I saw a small, black, disk-shaped object traveling north at a very high rate of speed (in a straight line) under the clouds. **Author's Note:** it is rare for a disk-shaped UFO to be observed black in color; this is more typical of the black triangles reported all over the world.

9/17/2012

Time: 20:30
City: Bangor
Craft Shape: Light
Duration of Sighting: 1 hour

———— SUMMARY ————

Three blinking lights in night sky of Bangor, Maine, helicopters searching the area.

Author's Note: another possible incident of military presence in conjunction with a UFO sighting.

9/16/2012

Time: 3:30
City: Sebago
Craft Shape: Unknown
Duration of Sighting: 1.5 hours

———— SUMMARY ————

Strange, slow-moving light over Sebago, Maine.

9/15/2012

Time: 8:24
City: Scarborough
Craft Shape: Oval
Duration of Sighting: 10 minutes

SUMMARY

Over thirty orange silent lights all grouped and traveling east at the same speed.

Author's Note: another massive fleet sighing. Over thirty silent lights!

9/4/2012

Time: 21:36
City: Woodville
Craft Shape: Light
Duration of Sighting: Short

SUMMARY

Bright light chasing flying squirrel at night!

Author's Note: could this be a BOL. Described typically, as very small in size and some reports suggesting that they are responsible for crop circle formations.

9/2/2012

Time: 19:52
City: Macias
Craft Shape: Light
Duration of Sighting: Short

SUMMARY

Vertical, silent orange—fiery spheres overhead.

Author's Note: vertical spheres were also reported during the famous 2008 Stephenville, Texas UFO sightings.

8/18/2012

Time: 20:50
City: Phillips
Craft Shape: Light
Duration of Sighting: 7 minutes

SUMMARY

Orange light appears, and then reappears in same "flight path" about 20 minutes later.

Author's Note: UFOs have been described as sometimes shimmering, almost translucent, and other times vanishing completely, much like the UFO reported at Loring AFB.

8/17/2012

Time: 21:00
City: York Beach
Craft Shape: Circle
Duration of Sighting: 10 minutes

—————— SUMMARY ——————

9 round, reddish lights in a long, straight row about 30 seconds apart, sighted by 7 visitors on York Beach.

Author's Note: a fleet and multiple witnesses!

8/16/2012

Time: 22:00
City: Small Point
Craft Shape: Sphere
Duration of Sighting: 2 minutes

—————— SUMMARY ——————

Orange-looking fireballs floating, dimming, and brightening, and making circular motions around each other before vanishing."

8/13/2012

Time: 20:45
City: Bangor
Craft Shape: Light
Duration of Sighting: 2 minutes

——— SUMMARY ———

Single light slowly moves across the horizon. (NUFORC Note: Possible sighting of ISS? PD)

Author's Note: viewing the (ISS) International Space Station is exciting, but all to often, it can be a misidentified UFO.

8/8/2012

Time: 21:50
City: North Anson
Craft Shape: Light
Duration of Sighting: 3 minutes

——— SUMMARY ———

High speed light that seemed to wobble!

8/7/2012

Time: 23:00
City: Old Orchard Beach
Craft Shape: Cross
Duration of Sighting: 3-5 minutes

SUMMARY

A florescent, orange-glowing cross-shaped craft with glowing yellow aura, moving slowly across the sky, low altitude.

8/7/2012

Time: 21:30
City: Augusta
Craft Shape: Circle
Duration of Sighting: 3-5 minutes

SUMMARY

Disc/ball-shaped object crossed the skyline faster than a conventional aircraft and returned slowly, with no sound.

7/28/2012

Time: 21:15
City: Cornish
Craft Shape: Circle
Duration of Sighting: 3-5 minutes

SUMMARY

A row of horizontal yellow/orange lights hovering over the Saco River.

Author's Note: often, a "row" of lights is simply based on perspective. Some of the video footage of the Phoenix Lights looks like a horizontal row of lights, however, once the perspective changes, even slightly, a boomerang shape revealed itself. Could be similar to this sighting.

7/20/2012

Time: 4:00
City: Greene
Craft Shape: Diamond
Duration of Sighting: 2 hours

SUMMARY

A diamond-shaped craft grows brighter, vanishes and comes back, hovering in the distance in Greene, Maine.

Author's Note: anytime I read reports of a diamond-shaped UFO, I think of the famous Cash-Landrum encounter that occurred in 1980. While driving along a highway, people viewed a large, diamond-shaped UFO shooting flames from its bottom. At one point, they stopped the vehicle and Betty Cash stepped out of the car. After some time, helicopters descended upon the craft and all flew away together. Immediately following the incident, all witnesses, (there were three in the car that night) suffered from radiation poisoning. To read the entire, incredible story please visit: http://www.ufocasebook.com/Pineywoods.html.

7/16/2012

Time: 0:00
City: Sanford
Craft Shape: Triangle
Duration of Sighting: 4-5 minutes

SUMMARY

Low flying, low speed stealth military aircraft.
Author's Note: Stealth Bomber?

7/9/2012

Time: 23:00
City: Bangor
Craft Shape: Other
Duration of Sighting: 20-60 seconds

SUMMARY

Stubby boomerang-shaped object with no lights, tan/orange in color.

7/7/2012

Time: 22:15
City: Portland
Craft Shape: Sphere
Duration of Sighting: 20 minutes

SUMMARY

8+ orange lights moving swift and silent in the night.

6/23/2012

Time: 21:00
City: Camden
Craft Shape: Fireball
Duration of Sighting: 1 hour

SUMMARY

About thirty bright orange lights drifted slowly east and rose upwards over Camden, Maine, between 9 p.m. and 10 p.m. June 23rd, 2012.

Author's Note: another fleet sighting, however, based on the time of year, and the calendar of events that take place in Camden during the summer, this could have been a release of Chinese Lanterns.

4/19/2012

Time: 20:42
City: Scarborough
Craft Shape: Circle
Duration of Sighting: 9 minutes

SUMMARY

Five bright orange lights moving through sky from due east to due north; disappeared in sequence.

Author's Note: flares perhaps? Which was the same, "official" resolution provided in the Phoenix Lights case.

4/18/2012

Time: 23:30
City: Harpswell
Craft Shape: Sphere
Duration of Sighting: 1 hour

SUMMARY

Ball of pinkish-orange light over water that was stationary/hovering, leaving reflection in water, and then eventually receding.

Author's Note: possible USO?

3/30/2012

Time: 2:15
City: West Newfield
Craft Shape: Other
Duration of Sighting: 5 minutes

SUMMARY

Tethered satellites over Maine? Silver thread connection clearly visible.

Author's Note: tethered satellites, or space tethers are usually very long cables which are typically used for stabilizing or maintaining the formation of specific space systems for trajectory coordination.

3/22/2012

Time: 1:00
City: Presque Isle
Craft Shape: Triangle
Duration of Sighting: 2 minutes

SUMMARY

Two amber-colored objects appeared to be playing in the air, darting back and forth at high rates of speed.

3/6/2012

Time: 15:50
City: Loring
Craft Shape: Cylinder
Duration of Sighting: 10 minutes

SUMMARY

70 witnesses close to Old Loring Air Force Base in Maine observed a right-circle cylinder-shaped object w/wings on either side.

Author's Note: 70 witnesses?!?! Did Loring's visitors from 1975 come back?

1/28/2012

Time: 22:00
City: Gorham
Craft Shape: Disk
Duration of Sighting: 25 seconds

SUMMARY

Bright light flashes in sky, followed by a flying disk in Gorham, ME.

12/11/2011

Time: 7:18
City: Saco
Craft Shape: Formation
Duration of Sighting: 10 minutes

SUMMARY

Family driving around viewing Christmas lights in their neighborhood observed a bright, white, pulsating light.

Author's Note: to read the entire encounter please visit: http://www.nuforc.org/webreports/086/S86533.html.

9/25/2011

Time: 23:40
City: Phillips
Craft Shape: Light
Duration of Sighting: A few seconds

SUMMARY

Very large light moving across the sky, disappearing behind the tree line, followed by a flash of light as if something had exploded.

Author's Note: could be similar to a recent report from April of 2013 in Texas where video was taken of a potential UFO exploding in midair. To view the video, please visit: http://www.youtube.com/watch?v=ghN4zh28Wrs.

9/1/2011

Time: 21:00
City: Bernard
Craft Shape: Fireball
Duration of Sighting: 1-2 minutes

SUMMARY

A bright orange fireball traveled very slowly, taking 1-2 minutes, from east to west over Bass Harbor before burning itself out.

Author's Note: a friend of mine reported to me, that he saw a fireball in Southwest Harbor in 1995, which is very close to the town of Bernard.

8/15/2011

Time: 23:00
City: Kittery Point
Craft Shape: Triangle
Duration of Sighting: About a minute

SUMMARY

I noticed a strange plane and pointed at it; it then turned and flew directly over me and two friends—it was very low.

Author's Note: interesting how this report describes the UFO "noticing" the witness. Similar to the event Kenos experienced in Starks.

8/1/2011

Time: 4:30
City: Poland
Craft Shape: Circle
Duration of Sighting: 5 minutes

SUMMARY

Bright white ball in the sky that stopped and changed direction ninety degrees—airplanes can't do that.

6/20/2011

Time: 22:00
City: Naples
Craft Shape: Unknown
Duration of Sighting: 30-40 seconds

SUMMARY

Fishing remote pond in Canoe, observed bright light moving across sky that slows, stops, and disappears.

Author's Note: remote pond in a canoe...sounds like the start to the Allagash Abductions . . .

11/12/2010

Time: 18:30
City: Harrison
Craft Shape: Triangle
Duration of Sighting: 5 minutes

SUMMARY

Red tipped UFO over Route 35 in Harrison, Maine.

9/24/2010

Time: 19:45
City: Kennebunkport
Craft Shape: Other
Duration of Sighting: 15 to 20 minutes

SUMMARY

Thirty craft with orange lights passed overhead in Kennebunkport, Maine.
Author's Note: another fleet sighting!

8/13/2010

Time: 21:30
City: Eagle Lake
Craft Shape: Circle
Duration of Sighting: 20 minutes

SUMMARY

Circular craft that had lights making a full circle, and large dome light in center.

Author's Note: while common in the golden era of UFO sightings, rarely do we see UFOs reported with a dome. To view a picture of a classic dome UFO please visit: http://www.uforth.com/banner/disc1.jpg

MUTUAL UFO NETWORK (MUFON) MAINE REPORT INDEX

Each of the following reports will show:
Line 1: Date reported, date of event, time
Line 2: Location in Maine
Line 4: Short Description

Winter and Spring 2013

Date Reported: 06/05/2013
Date of Event: 06/04/2013
Time: 00:00
Location: Bangor

SUMMARY

Large, bright, white light, 500+feet above the tree line moving from south to east.

Date Reported: 06/04/2013
Date of Event: 06/04/2013
Time: 21:30
Location: West Paris

SUMMARY

Orange Ball with bright flame of red glowing light. Flew straight and got smaller as it flew away.

Author's Note: though reported as an orange ball, the flame piece is often misidentified jets using afterburners.

Date Reported: 06/04/2013
Date of Event: 06/04/2013
Time: 09:30
Location: Chesterville

SUMMARY

Bright white light, no sound, light gray beams.

Author's Note: please view the entire report for more info on the "light gray beams": http://mufoncms.com/cgi-bin/report_handler.pl?req=view_long_desc&id=47872&rnd=.

Date Reported: 05/18/2013
Date of Event: 03/17/2013
Time: 23:30
Location: Portland

SUMMARY

Low-floating round object glowing yellow/orange, hovered with a few bobbing actions for about three minutes. Floated SE direction before it disappeared as if extinguished.

Author's Note: interesting how its disappearance was described as "extinguished." All too often, reports indicate that UFOs will vanish, implode, or cloak themselves. Extinguished is a great descriptor.

Date Reported: 05/17/2013
Date of Event: 05/17/2013
Time: 21:15
Location: Portland

SUMMARY

Bright orange light southwest of Portland, Maine. Appeared to be traveling northeast for several seconds, stopped hovered, burst out. Observed dark object descending straight down with aid of binoculars.

Author's Note: again, interesting description with "burst out." Perhaps describing a quick acceleration.

Date Reported: 04/29/2013
Date of Event: 04/27/2013
Time: 20:15
Location: Exeter

SUMMARY

A bright light in the sky; thought it was a plane on fire.

Author's Note: the fire description could indicate that this was a meteor, but in viewing the picture, the object is certainly peculiar. To view the picture please visit: http://www.mufoncms.com/files/47067_submitter_file1__001.JPG.

Date Reported: 04/28/2013
Date of Event: 04/28/2013
Time: 09:00
Location: Lisbon

SUMMARY

Bright red light came above tree line; 2 other objects followed, then all disappeared.

Date Reported: 04/22/2013
Date of Event: 04/21/2013
Time: 00:00
Location: Portland

SUMMARY

Five sets of lights from NE ascending. 2 pair and 1 trailing. All ascended and disappeared.

Date Reported: 03/26/2013
Date of Event: 01/08/2008
Time: 00:00
Location: Chelsea

SUMMARY

It was a saucer shape with circle windows in red and white and red flasher under. Looked grayish to silver surface.

Author's Note: a rare sighting with viewing actual windows on the craft. A famous sighting from Kumburgaz, Turkey, filmed by Dr. Roger Leir, showed not only windows, but biological entities inside. You can view one of these photos here: http://3.bp.blogspot.com/-FPQor7mY_6Q/TbbA8aodomI/AAAAAAAAAAQ/mbRJKEmOFUo/s1600/04.jpg.

Date Reported: 01/29/2013
Date of Event: 08/10/2011
Time: 20:00
Location: Casco

SUMMARY

Silent, large, black triangle, hovering slowly tree-top level, then became invisible.

Author's Note: another black triangle, typically regarded as military stealth amongst Ufologists.

Date Reported: 01/09/2013
Date of Event: 01/07/2013
Time: 00:00
Location: Dexter

SUMMARY

A round red object appeared at tree level. It was very close, glowing red. It hovered then started traveling west.

The Mutual UFO Network (MUFON) was created in 1969 as a non-profit organization to investigate the UFO phenomena. MUFON's mission statement is "The Scientific Study of UFOs for the Benefit of Humanity." Today MUFON continues to grow internationally and is the largest and most recognized UFO organization in the world. MUFON has a state director in each of the 50 states and 36 National Directors internationally, as well as over a thousand Field Investigators worldwide. MUFON through its recently formed MUFON Science Review Board (SRB) scans all incoming UFO cases and assembles a list each month of Cases of Interest. Every effort is made to bring these cases to a conclusion with the more important cases being reviewed by the SRB. For those cases that demand a more intense and immediate investigation, MUFON has organized a STAR Team where investigators can be at the site of the UFO event within 24 to 48 hours. Membership continues to grow annually both domestically and internationally with the addition of focus groups like the Abduction Research Team and other areas of interest. Anyone interested in joining MUFON, or becoming a MUFON FI is invited to join us at mufon.com.

GLOSSARY

ALIEN ABDUCTION: Taken against one's will, allegedly by extraterrestrial beings or craft. The experience is typically described as unpleasant, including odd medical procedures being performed on the abducted.

ALIEN IMPLANT: An object placed in one's body during an alien abduction medical procedure.

AMPHIBIOUS FAERIE: A mischievous, typically imaginary, being able to sustain life on both land and water.

AREA 51: A remote detachment of Edwards Air Force Base. It is located in the southern portion of Nevada in the western United States, 83 miles north-northwest of Las Vegas.

BATTLE OF LOS ANGELES: The name given to a supposed enemy attack, including U.S. anti-aircraft artillery rounds being fired at an object of unknown origin, typically being described as an extraterrestrial aircraft. The attack took place in Los Angeles, California, February 24, 1942.

BIGFOOT: An ape-like cryptid that purportedly inhabits forests, mainly in the Pacific Northwest region of North America. Bigfoot is usually described as a large, hairy, bipedal humanoid. The term "Sasquatch" is an anglicized derivative of the Halkomelem word sásq'ets

BOB LAZAR: A person who claimed to have worked at Area 51 as a scientist and an expert in extraterrestrial technology, due to his working on alien aircraft at the controversial facility.

CHUPACABRA: A cryptid said to inhabit parts of North and South America. The name comes from the animal's reported habit of attacking and drinking the blood of livestock, especially goats.

CLOSE ENCOUNTER: An event described when a person witnesses a UFO.

CROP CIRCLES: Typically described as an area of crops that were flattened in geometric patterns, believed to have been done by extraterrestrials.

DISTANT ENCOUNTERS: Described as, and includes, unexplainable light sources at night, oval- or disc-shaped objects sighted during the daytime or unidentified "blips" on radar screens that coincide with and confirm simultaneous visual sightings of UFOs.

EMF: Electromagnetic field. A physical field produced by electrically charged objects. It affects the behavior of charged objects in the vicinity of the field. The electromagnetic field extends indefinitely throughout space and describes the electromagnetic interaction.

EXTRATERRESTRIAL: Originating, existing, or occurring outside the earth or its atmosphere.

FEAR CAGE: A term used to describe a confined area with very high EMF readings.

FLATWOODS MONSTER: An alleged extraterrestrial encounter in the town of Flatwoods, West Virginia, on September 12, 1952.

FLYING HUMANOIDS: Considered to be a new phenomenon. In 2004, people have observed, photographed, and even videotaped the appearance of unidentified flying objects in the shape of humans. Some have been described as demons in flight. One tape shows an object described as "yeti-like" flying over the observer.

INDRID COLD: Eyewitnesses believe that Indrid Cold is one of the mysterious Men in Black, an alien, some other unknown creature, or all of the above, originally brought to attention from famed author John A. Keel in his book, *The Mothman Prophecies*.

MAINE MONSTER: The "Maine Monster" was a media sensation, making international news and spawning speculation. While some claimed that the animal was unknown (or a "mutant hybrid"), others suspected it was just an unusual-looking dog. When Maine monster hunter Loren Coleman was shown a photo of the creature on August 13, 2006, he stated, "This is a dog, probably a feral dog or a hybrid, but a dog."

MANNA MACHINE: Believed by ancient alien theorists to be a machine made by aliens and humans to create a type of algae as a food source used by the Israelites to help them survive their forty years in the Sinai Desert.

MEN IN BLACK: Usually refers to members of the FBI, CIA, NSA, or any members of other covert, government run, or para-military organization or the organizations themselves. These organizations are sometimes involved with extraterrestrial or other worldly matters.

MOTHMAN: A cryptid first reported in the Point Pleasant, West Virginia area from November 15, 1966 to December 15, 1967.

ORANG PENDEK: A cryptid that is reported to inhabit areas of the island of Sumatra.

PARANORMAL: Beyond the range of normal experience or scientific explanation.

PROJECT BLUE BOOK: The study of UFOs conducted by the United States Air Force from 1952-1969.

RENDLESHAM FOREST ENCOUNTER: The December 1980 encounter of unexplained lights and the landing of a possible alien spacecraft in Rendlesham Forest, Suffolk, England, which was investigated by United States soldiers who were stationed at the base.

ROSWELL UFO CRASH: A UFO allegedly crashed on a ranch near Roswell, New Mexico, July 7, 1947.

SKYWATCH: To monitor the sky for aircraft or any objects of potential unknown origin.

THE ALIEN SKELETON FROM MEXICO: Found in a barn in 2007, it is believed that a tiny alien was found alive. Subsequent DNA testing has proved the skeleton to be nothing more than a squirrel monkey. Also, a confession has since come forward claiming that this was, in fact, a hoax perpetrated by Taxidermist Urso Ruiz.

UFO (UNIDENTIFIED FLYING OBJECT): An unexplained object seen in the sky.

USO (UNIDENTIFIED/UNDERWATER SUBMERGED OBJECT): An unexplained object seen underneath, flying out, or into the water.

VIMANAS: Flying machines as described in the Sanskrit epics.

BIBLIOGRAPHY

"1975 Loring AFB UFO—A Son Tell's Father's Story." 1975 Loring AFB UFO - A Son Tell's Father's Story. Ed. Brian Vike. Rense.com, 17 Oct. 2006. Web.

"A Visit to the Doctor." The Cosmic Jokers. Grayalien.com, n.d. Web.

"Area 51." Wikipedia. Wikimedia Foundation, 06 Feb. 2013. Web.

"Electromagnetic Field." Wikipedia. Wikimedia Foundation, n.d. Web. 03 June 2013.

"Extraterrestrial Definition." Merriam-Webster. Merriam-Webster, n.d. Web.

"Flying Humanoids Definition." Seadict.com. N.p., 2012. Web.

"Interesting Facts About UFOs & Aliens." New Realities. N.p., 17 Dec. 2009. Web.

"Men in Black Definition." UrbanDictionary.com. N.p., n.d. Web.

"MUFON Case Management System." MUFON.com. N.p.

"Paranormal Definition." TheFreeDictionary.com. N.p., n.d. Web.

"Untitled Document." MUFON.com. N.p., May 2011. Web.

Allen, Wendy C. For Fear Of Little Men. N.p.: Lulu Enterprises, 2011.

Association, American Psychiatric. Diagnostic and Statistical Manual of Mental Disorders: DSM-IV-TR. Washington, DC: American Psychiatric Association, 2000. Print.

Booth, B.J. "Allagash, The Event." CrowdedSkies.com. N.p., n.d. Web.

Coleman, Loren. "Maine UFO Researcher Shirley Fickett Passes." Maine UFO Researcher Shirley Fickett Passes. Rense.com, 5 Feb. 2005. Web.

Dash, Mike. Borderlands: The Ultimate Exploration of the Surrounding Unknown. N.p.: Overlook Hardcover, 1999. Print.

Fawcett, Lawrence, and Barry J. Greenwood. The UFO Cover-Up: What the Government Won't Say. New York: Prentice-Hall, 1984. Print.

Filer, George A. "Vivid UFO Sightings Including Huge Triangle Over Maine." Vivid UFO Sightings Including Huge Triangle Over Maine. Rense.com, n.d. Web. 16 Jan. 2001.

Fowler, Raymond E. The Allagash Abductions: Undeniable Evidence of Alien Intervention. Tigard, OR: Wild Flower, 1993. Print.

Gill-Austern, Maggie. "Flying Object Spooks Man" *Sun Journal* [Lewiston] 11 Nov. 2006: n. pag. Print.

Gill-Austern, Maggie. "Odd Lights, Low Sounds Cause Stir." *Sun Journal* [Lewiston] 14 Feb. 2007: n. pag. Print.

Gross, Patrick. "UFO Photographs." Ufologie.com. N.p., 15 May 2005. Web.

Hynek, J. Allen. *The UFO Experience: A Scientific Inquiry.* N.p.: Da Capo, 1998. Print.

Johnson, Donald A. "On This Day - July 22." UFO Info. UfoInfo.com, 18 July 2012. Web.

Kimball, Michael. "A Strange Light Over Starks Maine." *Yankee Magazine* Apr. 1982: n. pag.

Leir, Roger K. *Casebook: Alien Implants.* New York: Dell, 2000. Print.

Long Island Paranormal Investigators. "Paranormal Terms And Definitions." Liparanormalinvestigators.com. N.p., 2003. Web.

Maine UFO Hunter. "Maine UFO Video Part 1 of 2 (March 10th 2009) Rare." YouTube. YouTube.com, 23 Apr. 2009. Web.

Pfeifer, Ken. "Close Encounter Over Bucksport Maine." Global Paranormal. N.p., 5 May 2013. Web.

Pratt, Bob. "5 Weird-Looking Aliens Abduct Young Man." MUFON.com. N.p., n.d. Web.

Radford, Benjamin. "Mystery Monster Dogs Maine." LiveScience.com. N.p., n.d. Web. 24 Sept. 2006.

Randles, Jenny. *Alien Contacts & Abduction: The Real Story from the Other Side.* New York: Sterling, 1994. Print.

Schwarz, Berthold Eric. *UFO-dynamics: Psychiatric and Psychic Dimensions of the UFO Syndrome.* Moore Haven, FL: Rainbow, 1983. Print.

Smith, S.E., and Bronwyn Harris. "What Is an Unidentified Submerged Object?" WiseGeek. Conjecture, n.d. Web.

Spignesi, Stephen. *The UFO Book Of Lists.* N.p.: Citadel, 2000. Print.

State Report Index for Maine. Rep. N.p.: NUFORC, 2013. National UFO Reporting Center. Web.

Stevens, Alexander. "Allagash Aftermath." *North Shore Sunday* [Salem] 12 Sept. 1993, Arts & Leisure sec.: n. pag. Print.

Stevens, C.J. *The Supernatural Side of Maine.* N.p.: John Wade, 2002.

Print.

Strickler, Lon. "The Legendary Men in Black." Phantoms and Monsters. PhantomsandMonsters.com, Feb. 2012. Web.

Sweetman, Bill. "The Top-Secret Warplanes of Area 51." Popular Science. N.p., 1 Oct. 2006. Web.

Unknown. "Long Description of Sighting Report." MUFON. N.p., 29 Apr. 2013. Web.

Unknown. Recent UFO Sightings. Squido.com, Web.

Unknown. *Times Record* [Brunswick] 30 June 1971: n. pag. Print.

Vallee, Jacques. *Passport to Magonia*. N.p.: McGraw-Hill Contemporary, 1974. Print.

Ward, Kent. "The Loring UFO Episode Revisited." *Bangor Daily News* 3 Oct. 2009: n. pag. Print.

Webmaster, Caribou. "NOAA's NWS Forecast Office—Caribou, Maine—." NOAA's NWS Forecast Office—Caribou, Maine—. National Weather Service, 18 Jan. 2007. Web

Webmaster, GUFON. "GUFON - Global UFO Network." GUFON - Global UFO Network. Global UFO Network, 2005. Web.

INDEX

Allagash, 11, 40, 42, 43, 128
Allen Street, 55
Androscoggin River, 64
Bachelder Brook, 86
Bangor, 7, 62, 73, 75, 83, 97, 98, 99, 103, 113, 117, 121, 132
Bar Harbor, 13, 62
Bath Iron Works, 54, 55, 79
Berwick, 55, 103,
Big Black River, 15
Blue Hill, 61
Boothbay Harbor, 61
Bowdoin College, 53
Brann Mills Road, 56
Brunswick, 26, 27, 53, 54
Brunswick Naval Air Station, 48, 52, 53, 67
Bucksport, 75
Close Encounter, 26, 30, 31, 42, 68, 90, 91
Conversion Disorder, 19
Cook's Corner, 53
Custom House Street, 20
Depot Mountain, 15
Distant Encounters, 30, 90
Dr. Herbert Hopkins, 34
Dr. Roger Leir, 31, 136
EMF, 22, 23, 25, 139
Eagle Lake, 11, 40, 130
East Newport, 77, 95
Ellsworth, 13, 61, 102
Exeter, 83, 84, 134
Farmington, 58, 67
Fear Cage, 22, 139
Fort Kent, 10, 11, 15
Franklin County, 64, 67
Freeport, 22, 24, 96, 105, 112
Frenchman's Bay, 13
Gardiner, 80, 81, 82
Haynesville Road, 11
Industry, 64, 66, 67
J. Allen Hynek, 29
Kennebec River, 55, 64
Lake Thompson, 32
Leland Bechtel, 67

Loring Air Force Base, 11, 27, 32, 46, 47, 48, 49, 50, 51, 53, 116, 125
Madison, 58, 59
Man in Black, 33, 37, 38
Men in Black, 7, 29, 36, 50, 139
Mount Desert Island, 13
Mud Brook Campsite, 40
New Sharon, 59
North Whitefield, 68
Northeast Harbor, 13
Northern Maine, 13, 14, 15, 40
Norway, 32, 33, 34
Old Brunswick Road, 22
Old Orchard Beach, 35, 36, 39, 85, 118
Oxford, 32
Paranormal, 7, 10, 11, 13, 14, 18, 20, 22, 24, 28, 44, 59, 67, 77, 88, 89, 140
Poland, 32, 128
Police, 33, 34, 47, 48, 53, 55, 59, 60, 61, 67, 80, 94, 104
Portland, 18, 20, 43, 105, 122, 133, 134, 135
Rangeley Lake, 64
Ross Forest, 85, 86
Route 1, 11, 22, 27, 97
Route 26, 32
Route 43, 57, 58
Route 46, 75
Saint John St., 18
Security Option 3, 46, 48
Shirley Fickett, 33, 34, 35, 37, 39
Somesville, 61
St. Francis, 11
St. John River, 16
Starks, 56, 58, 59, 60, 127
Timber Lake, 63
Trenton, 62
Tripp Pond, 33
USO, 75, 76, 123, 140
W.L. Blake Building, 20
WCSH 6, 43
Waterville, 60, 107, 108
Westbrook, 71, 72